FLEEING NAZI GERMANY

FIVE HISTORIANS MIGRATE TO AMERICA

ALLAN MITCHELL

Order this book online at www.trafford.com
or email orders@trafford.com

Most Trafford titles are also available at major online book retailers.

Printed in the United States of America.

ISBN: 978-1-4269-5536-5 (sc)
ISBN: 978-1-4269-5537-2 (hc)
ISBN: 978-1-4269-5538-9 (e)

Library of Congress Control Number: 2011901035

Trafford rev. 02/12/2011

 www.trafford.com

North America & international
toll-free: 1 888 232 4444 (USA & Canada)
phone: 250 383 6864 ♦ fax: 812 355 4082

TABLE OF CONTENTS

PREFACE

The autobiographical form is fraught with pitfalls. Unavoidably, when attempting to summarize one's own life, there is a tendency by authors either to suppress certain compromising details or to exaggerate the significance of those presented. The very nature of the enterprise necessarily precludes any claim to objectivity. By definition, then, the end product can only be personal and, to a greater or lesser degree, narcissistic. Hence it is unsurprising to find in memoirs several or all of the same characteristics: self-congratulation, name-dropping, all too frequent references to "my friend" so-and-so, inflated claims of prescience, sententious lessons from some fortuitous twist of fate, unduly elaborate efforts to integrate particular experience with general history, and so on. Yet arguably these recurrent traits of most autobiographical writing should be accepted and indeed relished by readers, since they lend such accounts their individual flavor.

This study is based largely on five published autobiographies that share a common set of themes. All were composed by persons who were born in Germany before 1933, who left their native land during the opening years of the Nazi regime, and who subsequently established outstanding academic careers in the United States as historians of Europe. Admittedly, this is but a tiny sample of the thousands of European intellectuals who fled from fascism to America, but there is surely value in examining carefully the various cases of the scholars who have been chosen to represent the rest.

In general, this remarkable tale of migration in the 1930s is a topic already well explored. It is conspicuous, however, that the best broad-gauged survey of the subject by H. Stuart Hughes includes no category for historians and makes no mention of the five names that primarily figure here.[1] Even the extensive compendium of refugee historians published by Catherine Epstein confines itself to what she calls "the first generation," that is, those persons who had already completed their academic training in Germany and who thus arrived in America as adults.[2] A survey of the second generation, those who came to the United States as children or teenagers, has been compiled by the Swiss researcher Heinz Wolf, but it was released long before the most recent wave of relevant memoirs appeared at the turn of the twenty-first century.[3] Five of these latecomers are to be considered in the pages following. Only one of them, Felix Gilbert, has been selected to stand in for the first generation; the others, whose autobiographies have more recently been issued in print, properly belong to the second. Their stories deserve our attention as well.

While exposing the criteria for concentrating on these five, in the interest of full disclosure, a personal word at the outset is appropriate. As it happened, I came to know each of them, more or less well, in the course of my own career. Two were only incidental acquaintances: Felix Gilbert, who was a visiting lecturer at Harvard during my graduate studies there; and Peter Gay, whom I first met at Yale and who later visited me at UC San Diego as keynote speaker at a colloquium I had organized for the retirement of my senior colleague Stuart Hughes. Two were close friends: Klemens von Klemperer, my long-time neighbor and faculty colleague at Smith College; and Werner ("Tom") Angress, with whom I often exchanged family outings on Long Island and in Berlin. Fritz Stern fell somewhere between on this scale of familiarity as an individual with whom I shared intellectual pursuits in New York and Germany. I may append the observation, which should become evident, that these various friendships did not entirely dull my critical spirit and that it is far from my intention to indulge here in hagiography. Rather, as an American, I have attempted to draw fair portraits of these five refugee scholars and, in the concluding chapter, to derive apt generalizations, comparisons, and contrasts.

One final prefatory remark is essential. The historians under discussion are introduced according to their age, starting with the eldest, Felix Gilbert, born before 1914, and ending with the youngest, Fritz Stern, who was barely six years old when Adolf Hitler became the German chancellor in January 1933. The other three experienced the advent and expansion of Nazism as children maturing into their teens. All were thoroughly German as youngsters, and all later became perfectly fluent in their adopted English language during the later American phase of their lives. Yet a word of caution is required in specific reference to their Jewishness, a subject to which we must return. To speak flatly of "five Jews" in this instance would be to adopt the Nazi blanket definition of that term and to deny the individuality on which every autobiographer has a right to insist.

As always, a few friends deserve my inadequate expression of gratitude for helping me to prepare the manuscript: Stanley Chodorow, Peter Hennock, Larry Joseph, Annemarie Kleinert, Mili Rapp, and Tom Skidmore.

Chapter One

FELIX GILBERT

Born in 1905 at Baden Baden, where his father was a physician and director of a tuberculosis sanatorium, Felix Gilbert was perfectly representative of the elder generation of German-bred scholars who experienced the Nazi regime after 1933 as young adults and who left their native land to pursue a professional career in the United States. His father was the son of a British officer – hence the name Gilbert – who married a woman from the Rhineland and then settled with her in Germany, where Felix's father grew up and gained his medical training. Tragically, the latter died prematurely a few months after the birth of his son, and the young widow Gilbert moved soon thereafter to Berlin. As an adult Felix Gilbert liked to claim that he hailed from Baden, but the truth was that he always spoke German with a distinct Berlin accent.[4]

The extensive family of Gilbert's mother is far more difficult to untangle. Its deep historical roots stretched back to the Enlightenment philosopher Moses Mendelssohn and to the much celebrated composer

1

of the early nineteenth century Felix Mendelssohn-Bartholdy. Another branch bore the name of Oppenheim, a distinguished wealthy Jewish banking dynasty in Berlin. In addition, one must take account of a Prussian army officer, a professor of medicine at the University of Berlin, and a grandfather who founded the prosperous chemical and photo firm of AGFA, which eventually became a major element of the giant industrial conglomerate I. G. Farben. Ever discreet, Gilbert makes no mention in his memoirs of the awful irony that I. G. Farben produced much of the toxic gas used by the Nazis in their extermination camps.[5]

This cursory review is sufficient to establish that Felix Gilbert was the scion of a cosmopolitan and quite well-to-do clan that securely occupied a privileged rank in Berlin's upper bourgeoisie, a social class that was coming to prominence and political clout in the wake of national unification in 1870. Gilbert's boyhood thus coincided with the glory days of the German Kaiserreich and, though he never uses the term, he was unmistakably an offspring of the Belle Époque. That term is all the more appropriate since the combination of money and education meant among other things that the command of foreign languages was taken for granted in the family. Gilbert had an English governess (who left just before the outbreak of war in 1914), and he was exposed to regular French lessons, a tongue spoken fluently by his mother. Another family trait is worth emphasizing. Although everyone was fully aware of their Jewish background, the Mendelssohns had converted to Lutheranism in the early nineteenth century. Moreover, because of frequent intermarriages with Christians, the religious identity of the family had become so blurred by the prewar years that Felix Gilbert matured in an atmosphere thoroughly secular, conservative, and patriotic. To this summary we may append a further symptomatic note: one of his uncles, Otto Mendelssohn Bartholdy, after making a substantial contribution to the construction of a memorial church (*Gedächtniskirche*) to Kaiser Wilhelm I in downtown Berlin near the Kurfürstendamm, was ennobled by Wilhelm II. Felix himself inherited no title, but he did receive all the trappings of a successful and well connected German family.[6]

As a child Gilbert's beat extended from that Gedächtniskirche (now only a jagged remnant) though Dahlem and Grunewald to Charlottenburg. At the time, the latter was still a separate and somewhat bucolic settlement west of Berlin that served as a summer residence for the city's nobility and bourgeois elite. Naturally his family was represented there, since his great-grandfather owned a residence at which Felix spent his vacations. Once that house was sold, Felix's mother ordinarily rented a dwelling in Rindbach, a village on the Traunsee in Austria, where he and his sister henceforth passed their summers. Young Felix thought the place much too remote and somewhat boring; later he found it difficult to overcome his distaste for Austria. While he remained a North German to the teeth, photos of him from that time have survived, clad in Lederhosen with suspenders and a Tyrolean hat, rather to his embarrassment. More compromising still, he had to confess to his American college students many years later that he once as a boy presented flowers to Kaiser Franz Joseph of the Habsburg Dual Monarchy, an admission that clearly dated him as someone who had lived before the First World War.[7]

In July 1914 Gilbert was vacationing with his immediate family at a seaside resort on the coast of the Netherlands when the news broke that a military conflict in Europe was imminent. They immediately caught a train back to Germany – the last time, he recalled, Gilbert crossed an international border without any passport control.[8]

Initially life continued much as before. At the outset of the war Gilbert was nine years old and soon enrolled in a Berlin Gymnasium. By the war's end he was thirteen and, while pursuing his studies, he noticed little change from prewar circumstances despite the insurrectionary events of 1918. In Berlin there was no physical destruction and precious little social upheaval. One incident, however, stuck vividly in mind. On his daily walk from school to home he came one day to the Landwehrkanal, where a crowd had gathered. A corpse was being fished out of the water: the body of Rosa Luxemburg, the Spartacist leader who was assassinated along with Karl Liebknecht by rightist militants. Although he regretted such violence, Gilbert was nonetheless relieved that the threat of a Communist putsch had thereby been thwarted.[9] In general, not surprisingly, the war years had brought out in him a markedly patriotic streak. He remembered, whenever the announcement of a great German victory occurred, that he and his playmates would gather before the Imperial Palace and sing nationalistic songs. At home he built tiny wooden ships and played with tin soldiers, even though he considered himself a pacifist. Yet he adored men in uniform. In short, Gilbert was a normal German youngster who was aware of his Jewishness (25 percent, he remarked) but who thought little or nothing of it. Two of his closest friends at the Friedrichs Werdersche Gymnasium were Jewish, but no one noticed or cared.

In his memoirs Gilbert conspicuously denies that a rising tide of anti-Semitism was noticeable during the First World War or as an immediate consequence of it.[10]

In 1923, at the age of eighteen, Gilbert began his university studies in Heidelberg. It proved to be a brief episode from which few memories remained. This was the period of Germany's great inflation, from which he was shielded after his rich uncle Otto von Mendelssohn-Bartoldy gave him a fifty dollar bill in US currency that lasted through the financial crisis with ten dollars to spare. At the university he shopped around, for example by attending the lectures of the noted philosopher Karl Jaspers and the sociologist Alfred Weber (brother of Max). He considered becoming a painter or a philosopher but soon settled on history as his *Hauptfach*. He also developed, given his decidedly conservative family background, surprisingly liberal political views. This tilt was not entirely new, since during the war he had openly supported the 1917 Reichstag resolution favoring peace without annexation, and he had opposed Germany's unrestricted submarine warfare against Allied shipping. Yet he despised the French occupation of the Ruhr in 1923 when he scornfully passed French soldiers guarding the bridges between Heidelberg and occupied Mannheim across the Rhine. At the conclusion of his first semester, while returning to Berlin, he stopped in Nürnberg and there saw for the first time a display of swastika flags during a Nazi party rally. He had at that time no reason to believe, Gilbert later commented, that Adolf Hitler would ever be of much significance.[11]

Back in Berlin, Gilbert obtained a junior position with an editorial team that was preparing the publication of *Die Grosse*

Politik, a collection of documents from the Second Reich's Foreign Office that was intended to disprove the infamous war guilt thesis that Germany bore a primary responsibility for the origins of armed conflict in 1914. Under the tutelage of a chief editor, Friedrich Thimme, young Felix Gilbert took over the section on the Berlin-Baghdad Railway, of which he remained inordinately proud. Among others, one of his collaborators was Hajo Holborn, an important historian of the same generation who later became a professor at Yale.[12] Meanwhile, public circumstances began to settle down: Communist agitation in Saxony and the Nazi putsch attempt in Bavaria were suppressed, the German Mark was stabilized, and the French Ruhr occupation was terminated. By the time Gilbert left his editorial post in 1925, things were looking up for Germany, although he still lacked confidence in the future stability of the Weimar Republic. "Nothing was certain."[13]

In the 1920s Gilbert was a man about town. In a metropolis like Berlin, he said, one could know only certain parts of it well, and "my Berlin was the bourgeois section of the city," meaning Unter den Linden westward as far as the Nikolassee, the Wannsee, and Potsdam. He lived, as in his childhood, on the Tirpitz-Ufer on the edge of the Tiergarten near the Lützowplatz, addresses well known to residents. His social life was centered in the area of the Gedächtniskirche, then a neighborhood of elegant shops, cafés, and restaurants as well as his favorite bar, the Jockey, conveniently located at a ten minutes' walk from his apartment.[14]

The university (now the Humboldt in what became East Berlin) was at the end of an easy ride by bus. There he became a student of Friedrich Meinecke, a centrist *Vernunftrepublikaner*, that is, one who thought it reasonable to support the Weimar form of democracy even without passionate devotion to it. Meinecke became the grand patron of German intellectual history and attracted a remarkable coterie of graduate students in Gilbert's peer group, several of whom later migrated to America (besides Holborn, for instance, Hans Rosenberg, Fritz Epstein, Dietrich Gerhard, Gerhard Masur, and Hans Rothfels).[15] Gilbert was not personally as close to Meinecke as some others, but he was importantly influenced by him. During his graduate training he spent a year in Munich and undertook several trips to Italy, thereby developing an enduring interest in study of the Renaissance. But Meinecke discouraged him from writing his doctoral dissertation in that field, steering him instead to a treatment of the eminent historian Johann Gustav Droysen and securing for him a position as editor of Droysen's papers. Yet it was the Italian Renaissance that was to become Gilbert's main field of research. Incidentally, while in Munich he saw posters announcing a speech by Hitler, recently released from his Landsberg prison, but considered it too inconsequential to attend.[16]

When he was carousing in Berlin speakeasies or riding about the city in his little Opel, a gift from his family, Gilbert managed to form an impressive array of friends and acquaintances. They notably included Eckart Kehr, a maverick scholar of immense reputation in contemporary history; Theodor Eschenburg, later a famous sociologist; Dietrich Bonhoeffer, then a student in theology and later a martyr among the opponents of Nazism; and also Gustav Stresemann, whom Gilbert experienced as a moving orator and dedicated republican whose sudden death while the foreign minister in 1929 was "a fatal blow to democracy in Germany."[17]

Parenthetically it is worthwhile to record Gilbert's first trip to Paris in 1926, an "utterly exciting" visit that made an overwhelming impression. Yet, if less beautiful than the French capital, Berlin seemed to him intellectually more stimulating, a city where one could hear lectures by Arnold Toynbee, Johan Huizinga, and André Gide; attend concerts and operas conducted by Wilhelm Furtwängler, Bruno Walter, and Otto Klemperer; or enjoy theater productions of works by modern playwrights such as Ernst Toller, Georg Kaiser, and Carl Zuckmayer – not to forget, inevitably, Brecht and Weill's *Dreigroschenoper*. He took them all in. This was the seemingly stable political climate, economic prosperity, and cultural flourish in which Felix Gilbert grew to maturity, until an inexorable downward spiral started in 1929.[18]

While completing his work on Droysen, Gilbert took occasional breaks for archival forays to Florence and Rome. Then, in the summer of 1932, he moved to Italy for nearly a year to devote his full time to the Renaissance. He spent the intervening Christmas vacation back in Berlin and was on a train returning to Rome in early January 1933 when he learned of the impending political maneuvers that would bring Adolf Hitler to power. That potentiality was confirmed a few weeks later. Gilbert thus observed the initial phase of Nazi *Gleichschaltung* from afar, following it through Italian newspapers and private correspondence. His reaction was twofold and somewhat self-contradictory. On one hand, as he emphasizes in his memoirs, the process of nazification was very gradual and there seemed to be no immediate reason to be unduly alarmed or to suspect the worst. Yet he was at the same time remarkably quick to realize that an academic career for him in Germany would probably be impossible under Nazi rule. Like many others, his being partly Jewish was no professional issue at all until the Nazis made it one. To put it another way, Gilbert concluded that Germany did not have a "Jewish question," as Hitler repeatedly claimed, but certainly it did have a Nazi question.[19]

Hence Felix Gilbert regained Berlin in June 1933 in a pessimistic frame of mind. He was there in that October when Hitler announced Germany's withdrawal from the League of Nations and abandonment of the European Disarmament Conference. Gilbert left at once for London, where he spent the next two and a half years in a "cheerless gray" exile, living in rented rooms, taking endless underground rides, running low on funds, and being offended by English snobbery. He was not the first foreigner to take refuge in the reading room of the British Museum, but he found in Britain distressingly little interest in the Renaissance. He also found the British confused and often misguided in their estimates of Nazi Germany. He did dabble a bit in politics and was attracted to the Fabian Society, thereby gaining an opportunity to hear and admire George Bernard Shaw. Likewise, he attended sessions at the House of Commons, where he listened to speeches by Stanley Baldwin and Winston Churchill. But he remained deeply troubled by the course of events on the Continent and felt hopelessly out of sorts with his existence in London. Miraculously, it seemed, he received in 1936 the offer of a temporary teaching position in southern California at Scripps College and immediately boarded a ship for the United States, convinced as he was that America was a land of far greater opportunity for an alien academic like himself. He thereupon left Europe, without anguish, to discover the New World.[20]

Felix Gilbert's transition to America was thus rapid and relatively painless. His personal experience of migration was different from many others who would follow in two crucial regards. First, he had been initially exposed to triumphant Nazism when he was an adult, when his intellectual interests were already formed, and when his choice of the career of a Renaissance scholar was instrumental in the decision to depart from Germany. Second, that departure was extraordinarily early, before the iron trap of persecution began to choke off the lives of German Jews. By the summer of 1937 Gilbert was fully persuaded that his future was in the USA. Crossing the country by car, he stood on a crest at the front range of the Colorado Rocky Mountains and looked out over the Great Plains. It gave him a sense of infinity – and of infinite possibilities – much the same as peering at the Pacific Ocean from the coast of California. What Germany had denied him, Felix Gilbert would find here.[21]

For the time being, arrangements were temporary. He accepted a job as research assistant at the Institute for Advanced Study in Princeton (where he would later become a professor at the School of Historical Studies). He was there when the war began in Europe and when the United States entered it in December 1941. Meanwhile, he obtained American citizenship and promptly secured a position as European analyst with the OSS, the government's intelligence and counter-espionage agency in Washington, D.C. In this capacity he sailed in 1944 on the *Queen Elizabeth*, now a troop ship, to Britain, landing near Glasgow and taking a train to London, where he settled into an office at Grosvenor Square. Once again he was riding the underground, but this time with more appreciation, since the tubes were the safest refuge from the V-1 rockets that randomly fell.[22]

His duties consisted mainly of writing reports about interviews with German POWs and refugees, an assignment that brought him into contact with budding historians like Arthur Schlesinger, Jr., and Leonard Krieger. The information gathered there solidified his notion that life for most Germans had gone on after 1939 without many noticeable changes, until of course Allied bombing began to take a heavy toll on the major cities and food shortages began to impinge on the population. Yet for the most part Gilbert's routine was boring, and he whiled away his evenings in London's pubs, carousing in a manner bound to remind him of his gin-soaked tour of Berlin's *Kneipen* nearly twenty years before.[23]

At the end of 1944 Gilbert became more actively involved with planning for a forthcoming Allied occupation of Germany and, specifically, mapping the potential distribution of sectors in Berlin. After the liberation of Paris that August, an OSS office was opened nearby the Champs-Élysées, and he was transferred there from March to May 1945. He lived in a small apartment in the Rue des Saints-Pères on the Left Bank, whence he walked every day across the Seine, through the courtyard of the Louvre (before the pyramid was built), and caught the metro up to his office. It was a most pleasant interlude, especially as he felt no desire whatever to follow Allied troops into Germany. Duty nonetheless called, and Captain Gilbert was transferred with the entire Reseach and Analysis team to OSS headquarters in Wiesbaden, where they took up residence in the Henkel champagne factory in which that beverage was free. Personally he preferred wine with his billiards and croquet matches. Again he was charged with interviewing many Germans, from which he surmised – contrary to the opinion often formed by the newspaper press – that the Allied campaign of denazification was being largely successful, if only because so many Germans were so eager to denounce each other.[24]

Gilbert had an opportunity to visit many of the major cities of the Rhineland and to witness the extent of their destruction. A few had been spared, including Baden Baden where he was born (he viewed his family home without emotion) and Heidelberg where he first started at the university.[25] A greater impression was created by his trip to Freiburg, severely damaged by a single air strike in late 1944, though the magnificent cathedral stood virtually untouched. His contacts at the university there and in Heidelberg showed a distinction between them. The pre-Nazi Heidelberg faculty had been far more liberal and pro-republican during the Weimar years, so that the fascist seizure of power had produced turmoil, dismissals, and retributions – all of which now needed to be undone. Freiburg, to the contrary, had always been more conservative and Catholic, with the result that fewer committed Nazis were required to replace its professors. In Freiburg Gilbert had an unproductive encounter with ex-rector Martin Heidegger, who remained blissfully unaware throughout their talk that his American army interlocutor was also a scholar who had in fact read the master's principal philosophical work, *Sein und Zeit*. Also Gilbert met with the noted military historian Gerhard Ritter, who cheerfully recounted his brief incarceration after the failed attempt on Hitler's life in July 1944 and his escape from captivity.[26] Among the contacts with political personalities Gilbert singled out Kurt Schumacher, the Socialist leader recently released from a long term in concentration camps, and Otto Grotewohl, soon to be a dignitary of the East German regime. Gilbert was attracted to neither.[27] Finally, his postwar reconnaissance of Germany was capped by a return to Berlin, the center of which he found utterly devastated. The area around the Gedächtniskirche, where he had roamed as a young man, was now unrecognizable. His memory of that time was jogged by attending a production at the Brecht Theater in East Berlin of the *Dreigroschenoper* in which some of the same actors appeared who had been on stage more than a decade earlier.[28]

There was never the slightest doubt that Felix Gilbert would return to the United States to take up the career that had been altered and delayed since 1933 but by no means aborted. It began with a long stint at Bryn Mawr College near Philadelphia and included guest professorships at Smith College, the University of California at San Diego, Stanford, and Harvard. Professor Gilbert also returned for one year to Germany as a lecturer at the University of Cologne.[29] All of which culminated with his appointment at Princeton's Institute for Advanced Study, from which he retired many years later. His memoirs contain scant reference to his illustrious professional life after 1945, perhaps out of modesty. Predictably, his publications centered on Renaissance Italy, particularly on themes related to his extensive study of Machiavelli and his long-time interest in the history of the Roman papacy.[30] As a result he received countless awards and honorary degrees in Italy and the United States as well as from the Free University of Berlin. Despite all the detours and disappointments, in sum, Felix Gilbert emerged relatively unscathed from the tumultuous events in the first half of the twentieth century. His memoirs accordingly contain very little of the strutting and fretting evident in some others. Rather, his account evinces a serenity and steadfastness of purpose that eased his passage between two worlds.

Chapter Two

KLEMENS VON KLEMPERER

What's in a name? In the case of Klemens von Klemperer, it seems, quite a lot. As it happened, his paternal grandfather, a Director of the Dresdner Bank, was ennobled by the Habsburg Monarchy in 1910. Thereupon Gustav Klemperer became Gustav Klemperer Edler von Klemenau. Although this appellation was a fanciful collage, out of it came the young Klemens von Klemperer, born only six years later. That little three-letter word between the two K's had enormous consequences for him. Put a bit too baldly perhaps, it meant that he grew up not as a Berlin Jew but as an Austrian aristocrat.[31]

Such a statement requires further explanation. Both sides of the family had Austrian roots. Grandfather Gustav had settled in Dresden's *Altstadt*, "where the elegant families lived," surrounded by a host of relatives. There he was appointed the Austro-Hungarian Consul General, a service that earned him the title of nobility. His son, Klemens's father, became in turn a wealthy industrialist, who started in an armaments factory and then moved to Berlin as the head of a locomotive firm. The infant Klemens was born there in November 1916 and crawled about in a spacious apartment at the corner of Viktoria and Tiergartenstrasse, where the windows looked out over the Siegesallee, a most elegant address.[32] The maternal grandparents, a wealthy brewery family, meanwhile occupied a huge mansion – the "Palais Kuffner," as it was called – at a park in the ritzy Vienna suburb of Döbling. Their four Berlin grandchildren often passed their summer vacations at this exclusive residence of the Kuffner clan in greater Vienna. Thus Klemens von Klemperer was from the beginning, both in Germany and Austria, "geared for life in a gilded world," one that came with nursemaids, servants, cooks, and gardeners.[33]

Little Klemens was exactly two years old when the First World War ended. Two months later the Spartacist uprising erupted in Berlin, when violence in the streets caused his mother to draw the drapes of their Tiergarten apartment. The story goes that this tiny child lifted them to have a peek outside and "I saw a machine gun trained on me." A large automatic weapon was deliberately pointed at him? Frankly, this tale sounds like a favorite albeit unlikely family apple polished up over the decades to great hilarity. At least it does clearly establish that Klemens von Klemperer grew to political consciousness in the troubled postwar turmoil of the Weimar Republic rather than the relatively placid and secure circumstances of the preceding German Empire. Accordingly, the self-image that suffuses his memoir is that of a boy maturing in a time of "extraordinary creativity and a pronounced sense of crisis and disorientation."[34]

Klemperer was baptized and raised as a Lutheran Protestant, though the family had Jewish origins in Vienna. Both sets of grandparents lived in a totally secular fashion without a trace of Jewish tradition at home. They formally observed the usual Christian, not Jewish, holidays. Indeed, the boy did not learn of his Judaic background until the age of ten, when his Dresden grandfather died and the funeral service was performed by a rabbi. At school he and his siblings were teased at times about being Austrian, not Jewish. It followed that Klemens was confirmed in Berlin's fabled Protestant Dreifaltigkeitskirche, as he noted, "very much *comme il faut.*" Add to this the daily surroundings of a rigidly patriarchal family, complete with austere father and compliant mother, and it is little wonder that his conservative instincts were honed at an early age.[35]

Most of the Weimar period revolved around the famous Collège Français, or Französisches Gymnasium, located on the Pariser Platz next to the Reichstag building on the banks of the Spree River. It was a school where Junkers and Jews commingled with others, undisturbed. Nearly all classes were conducted in French, exception made only for math, German literature, and gymnastics. The Klemperer pupil entered at the age of eight in 1924 and left with his baccalaureate degree (*Abitur*) exactly a decade later, soon after the Nazi seizure of power. The institutional continuity of these formative years, despite political upsets, suggests a basic solidity of this teenager, even though he professed a sense of uncertainty and interregnum that was all too justified by events. Understandably, he was hardly attracted to the blandishments of Nazism, repulsed as he was not only by blatant racism but also by any form of fanaticism at odds with his conservative upbringing. As a student he had two intellectual heroes: Friedrich Nietzsche and Stefan George. Inspired by them, he imagined the career of a poet. It is no unkindness to observe that, in the decision between poetry and history, he assuredly made the proper choice of profession.[36] Such reverie was in any event cut short on 30 January 1933 when Adolf Hitler's minions paraded with torches in hand by his school and his home. Klemperer's life was not immediately altered – his Gymnasium did not hoist a swastika but retained the Prussian flag – yet it soon became apparent that his future was unlikely to lie in fascist Germany. He would have to choose, as he later wrote, between an inner or outer emigration. Conformity with the new political order was not an option.[37]

In 1934 Klemens von Klemperer's father contrived to have him admitted to Oxford. In effect, this was already the beginning of his permanent exile from Germany, even though he did not quite realize that at the time, and it did not turn out as the family expected. "Difficult son" that he was, Klemperer left England almost immediately and took refuge with his mother's family in Vienna. "Because of my Jewish ancestry," he explained, "the academic career to which I aspired … was closed to me in Germany."[38] That pronouncement constituted a perfect non sequitur, of course, since it shed no light at all on the reasons for his flight from Oxford. Yet it is easily surmised that he regarded Austria as the remaining hope of the good Germany and that he intended, no less, to help preserve it. The move also allowed him to occupy comfortable quarters in the Döbling mansion and thereby to lay further claim to his Viennese heritage. His memoirs aspire to report on a "turbulent life" in Austria, but the evidence smacks rather of a meandering boy at loose ends, rudderless in "a world of transition and uncertainty." He mentions street brawls in the city, but it remains unclear precisely what role, if any, he played in them. He preferred in any case to write poetry, and he kept a diary. Conspicuously, there was no entry in it for the night of 11-12 March 1938, when the Austrian Chancellor Kurt von Schuschnigg announced on the radio that he would have to capitulate to German demands for the *Anschluss* of his country with the Third Reich. Four days later Hitler entered Vienna. Klemperer was now the helpless witness of mob scenes and rowdy celebrations. He had not joined in any organized resistance, but there could be no question that the rising tide of fascism had now lapped up on the shores of his youthful exile like some ugly oil slick.[39]

He would need to depart. To do so would require that arrangements be made by his father for an American visa, which had already been accomplished for the two other Klemperer sons. There were complications, however, requiring that Klemens travel to Berlin. When he returned to Vienna, he found a swastika flying above the Döbling house, which had been confiscated by the Nazis. Traveling once more back to Berlin, he narrowly escaped being drafted into the German army and managed to find a temporary haven in the Swiss Embassy. One of his last recollections of the German capital was *Kristallnacht*, 9-10 November 1938, when he observed shattered store fronts from a passing bus. Soon thereafter, with visa in hand, he took a train to Hamburg and boarded a steam vessel bound for the United States.[40]

Klemens Von Klemperer arrived at a New York dock, appropriately, on Thanksgiving Day 1938. It is also appropriate that three quarters of his memoir are devoted to the time after that date, since he swiftly found a niche in American academia and remained comfortably ensconced there for the next five decades. A first big break occurred already in the following April when he was awarded a Refugee Scholarship to Harvard University. The following years were thus spent agreeably in Cambridge, Massachusetts, on a campus that could not have been more hospitable for a bright and handsome young would-be scholar. It was an ideal setting to perfect his English language skills and to learn the rudiments of his future endeavor. As is inevitable at Harvard, he was in the meanwhile amply exposed to celebrities, among them the former Chancellor of Germany, Heinrich Brüning, who explained his unrealized plans for a middle European customs union – which Hitler was in effect creating by other means. His most important contacts were with noted historians: Hajo Holborn and Hans Rothfels (both immigrants of an older generation); John Finley and Crane Brinton (Harvard regulars); and especially Sidney B. Fay, who was later to become his *Doktorvater*. In the summers Klemperer whiled away his vacations on the Rhode Island coast at Newport and nearby watering holes. The gathering darkness of events in Europe, for instance the German occupation of Paris, hardly perturbed this pleasant orientation to the American way of life. Whatever pangs of homesickness or nostalgia he felt were not for Berlin but Vienna – ever the Austrian aristocrat. Like all immigrants from the Old World at that time, Klemperer was acutely aware of the dichotomy between his European roots and his adopted homeland, but he seemed to combine them harmoniously and without anguish. In the middle of May 1940 he made a telling entry into his diary: "I shall see Germany again – but will I recognize it? America has become my second *Heimat*."[41]

After Harvard, Klemperer volunteered for the United States army and reported to Fort Devens, Massachusetts. By the time he donned khaki, in February 1943, the Hinge of Fate was already beginning to turn. Anglo-American troops had invaded North Africa and the battle of Stalingrad was all but decided. The Allies were consequently starting to address the problems likely to be faced through an invasion of the Continent and, further on, during a postwar occupation of Germany. These considerations explain Klemperer's immediate transfer to Camp Ritchie in Maryland, where he was attached to a unit of German-speakers being trained for intelligence work. After two months of instruction and after becoming a naturalized American citizen in May 1943, he boarded a plane for Britain. Soon posted to London, he was assigned to General Eisenhower's SHAEF staff with an office near Trafalgar Square, later in Kensington. His duties concerned mostly the examination of captured German documents in an effort to reconstruct the structure of the *Wehrmacht* that was soon to be engaged in battle on the mainland. This moderate activity allowed leisure time, which he used to join a fancy officers' club near London's Westminster Abbey. Klemens von Klemperer's war was consequently rather quiet, with a touch of luxury. An exception to that rule occurred one evening in June 1944, while on temporary air reconnaissance duty, when he witnessed the first attacks of German V-1 rockets on London, a florid rooftop spectacle of "fiery tracers piercing the sky."[42]

Three months after D-Day, once Paris had been liberated in August 1944, Klemperer's unit was delegated to the French capital. Again his landing was luxurious, first at the exclusive Hotel Crillon on the Place de la Concorde, then in a somewhat more modest and smaller hotel near the Opéra. His stay in Paris coincided with the infamous Battle of the Bulge, during which he saw no combat. He was still in Paris on VE-Day in May 1945 and there took part in the wild celebration in the streets that was beamed in newsreels across the world.[43]

A final episode of military service required a few months in occupied Germany during the autumn of 1945. SHAEF headquarters were now relocated to the devastated city of Frankfurt and housed in an abandoned factory owned by the chemical cartel I.G. Farben. "The German question" was much on Klemperer's mind: how could the punishment of a deserved defeat be reconciled with feelings of sympathy for the country of one's birth? Surely there had been some righteous Germans among the many wicked. Physically as well as emotionally, an effort to aid the recovery and to help establish a stable democracy was bound to be a "gigantic problem." Klemperer was briefly involved with the preservation and ordering of captured documents from the German Foreign Office that were discovered in the Harz Mountains, moved to Marburg and then Kassel, and finally deposited with the Berlin Document Center at Tempelhof. This immense project required the services of numerous German personnel, and to supervise them became his responsibility.[44] As for the city of Berlin, he found it to be a "sea of ruins." When he attempted to revisit the house of his birth, Klemperer discovered the entire neighborhood completely destroyed and unrecognizable – except for one old plane tree under which he had played as a child. He no longer belonged there. Without regret, therefore, he returned to the United States in late 1945 on the troop ship *SS Ernie Pyle*.[45]

Klemens von Klemperer's reintroduction to academic life in America was painless and profitable. He already had firm ties to Harvard, so nothing seemed more natural than to return to that university to resume his studies. After three and a half years of hiatus in the army, his career could flourish along with the "ongoing process" of his Americanization. The self-presentation in his memoirs of one compelled to keep wandering is somewhat at odds with his actual experience as a well established student at Harvard and then as a tenured professor at Smith College. Living for more than half a century in the same charming little brick house on Washington Avenue in Northampton, Massachusetts, while raising a lovely family with his wife Betty, scarcely qualifies as the existence of a vagabond, even accounting for extended trips to Europe.[46]

Back at Harvard, Klemperer represented the GI-Bill generation that flooded American universities after the war. Although he was initially not drawn back to Europe in any literal sense, his studies, friends, and teachers gradually led him there. His acquaintances included future academic stars like McGeorge Bundy, H. Stuart Hughes, Hans Gatzke, and John Conway. He was particularly attracted by prominent émigrés from Europe, both political and academic, such as Heinrich Brüning, Kurt von Schuschnigg, Alexander Kerensky, Michael Karpovich, and Gaetano Salvemini. His most important contacts among historians were with his mentors Sidney B. Fay and William L. Langer. The central intellectual problem that emerged from his brush with this potpourri of luminaries was an attempt to sort out a legitimate conservative tradition from the "ugly distortion" of Nazism. That was the focus of his doctoral dissertation at Harvard, which became his first book, *Germany's New Conservatism*, published by Princeton University Press in 1957 after his move to Smith College.[47]

His long and satisfying Smith career began after completion of the Ph.D. in 1949. He was unbothered by teaching at a women's college, since it certainly ranked then as an elite institution and possessed an "excellent faculty" – although he does not call them by name, excepting the learned and witty Elizabeth Lee Gallaher (a Smith graduate and also a Harvard Ph.D.) who joined the Department of English Literature in 1952 and was married to him in the year following.[48] If there is a disappointment in Klemperer's memoir, it is his cursory treatment of Northampton and his experience as a faculty member of the school where he spent the better part of his life. Instead, he is more interested in recounting his various sojourns in Europe during the second half of the twentieth century. Four stand out.

Predictably, the first visit was to Vienna. In fact, three trips were undertaken by Klemens von Klemperer to Austria between 1951 and 1957: alone, accompanied by his wife Betty, and then a Fulbright year in 1957-58 with their two blond toddlers in tow. These excursions afforded an opportunity to revisit the old family estate at Döbling, still occupied by the American military command in the early 1950s, as well as nearby attractions in Germany such as Munich, Murnau, and the Starnbergersee. Furthermore, they led Klemperer to launch an intellectual venture into Austrian history through a biography of the conservative Catholic Chancellor Ignaz Seipel, who had presided over his rump republican state during the interwar years, that is, between the demise of the Habsburg Monarchy and the advent of Nazism. This appropriately sad and even somewhat negative monograph, which owed much to the autobiographical element of Klemperer's own youth, was later published (again at Princeton) in 1972.[49] The second European trek was to the University of Bonn, where Klemperer temporarily replaced the eminent German political scientist – and historian of the Weimar Republic – Karl Dietrich Bracher. This full academic year abroad brought once more to the surface Klemperer's rather morose musings about being a perpetual refugee, forever wandering. "Was my having settled down in New England only an illusion?" If so, that was certainly not evident to his Northampton friends for whom he seemed rather to personify the prototypical American college professor who, like many others, took an occasional trip to Europe. Nonetheless he maintained his doubts.[50]

In the mid-1970s the Klemperer family enjoyed another year across the ocean, this time at the recently founded Churchill College of Cambridge University. Living in a town called Cambridge was hardly novel for a Harvard man, and it was also "a wonderful time," though the circumstances were different. Cricket instead of baseball, for instance. More significantly, Klemperer was moved to begin a study of the German Resistance Movement. He was obviously riveted by that topic because of his affinity with the conservative character of its principal protagonists, notably including the central figure of Adam von Trott zu Solz, an Oxford graduate who returned to Germany and gave his life among others in opposition to Nazism. Again motivated by a compulsion to show that "righteous Germans had existed," this weighty book was unquestionably Klemperer's most profound and fully realized work. *German Resistance against Hitler: The Search for Allies Abroad, 1938-1945* was published by Oxford University Press in 1992.[51]

The final major foray was back to Berlin, as a guest of Germany's most prestigious think tank, the *Wissenschaftskolleg*, in the late 1980s. This stay offered a chance to finish the Resistance book and also to relive the scenes of Klemperer's childhood. The return did not recall particularly happy memories, it must be said, and he felt a certain alienation from a city so ceaselessly changing. "Somehow," he commented, "Berlin does not lend itself to nostalgia." Otherwise his account dwelt on sights familiar to any visitor before 1989: the Wall, Checkpoint Charlie, strolling in East Berlin, the palace of Sans Souci at Potsdam, and so on. The strange mixture of familiar remnants and garish urban renewal could not fail to arouse reflections on the troubled past of his native land: "Everyone concerned with Germany must come to terms with the legacy of unspeakable crimes committed during the Nazi time...."[52]

The concluding section of Klemens von Klemperer's recollections is given over to an extended commentary on outstanding intellectual personalities since the late nineteenth century who had helped to shape his own thought. The names are all famous. He singles out the influence of Friedrich Nietzsche, Max Weber, and especially Dietrich Bonhoeffer. Klemperer does not pretend to be a philosopher, and it cannot be claimed that he developed any original personal credo or overarching *Weltanschauung*. Yet a few fixed points do emerge from his attempt to summarize his life's work and striving, which may be reduced here to four.

First, as always, there is his inveterate defense of conservatism. Solely the definition of it is reformulated: "a preference for the familiar over the unfamiliar." That quote is altogether symptomatic of a person, despite all his professions of being a wandering refugee, who writes from the perspective of a privileged and secure position with a kind of unshakable stoicism and a sense of *noblesse oblige*.

Tellingly, it is not Rousseau but Edmund Burke to whom he refers as the ultimate lodestar of his thinking.[53]

This inclination is closely related to another. Klemperer ends by accepting paradox as an essential element of the human condition. Throughout his memoir there is much rumination about the inner conflict between his European past and his American present, two souls in one breast. But the impartial observer is more likely to be struck by his almost effortless reconciliation of them. In discussing this "dialectic" (he uses the word), it is a curiosity that he twice mentions Hegel but never Immanuel Kant, since his conception of the world is surely more Kantian than Hegelian. There is no great clash of opposites in the night, and one does not gain the impression that he lay awake worried about churning contradictions.[54]

A third factor, even though it is seldom mentioned, is Klemperer's increasing devotion to religion. "The religious sphere," he finally avows, "has sustained me more and more." And that religion is Protestant Christianity, not Judaism. He was raised, after all, in a family that had previously converted and that had, for the most part, renounced the Jewish legacy in all its forms. The cathedral and not the synagogue loomed in Klemperer's boyhood. His Jewishness was of interest to the Nazis, to be sure, but it had not been formative or determinant for a young man who could easily pass for an Austrian aristocrat and often did so. His ambiguity was therefore not self-induced; it was mandated by political developments that he neither controlled nor well understood. The accumulating wisdom of advancing age did nothing to change this religious disposition but only reinforced it.[55]

Finally, it followed that an inescapable "tragic element" permeated Klemperer's consciousness. In the end he reaches the unremarkable conclusion that "we are not masters of our destiny." He comes very close to sounding like Albert Camus as he expounds on the absurdity of our existence – a notion, characteristically, in which he finds no contradiction with his religious convictions.[56] Ever the Kantian at heart, Klemens von Klemperer managed to survive the European tragedy of his time. "Who speaks of victory?" wrote the German poet Rainer Maria Rilke. "Survival is everything."

Chapter Three

WERNER T. ANGRESS

Something of a rarity among migrant scholars from Europe, the memoir of Werner T. Angress was originally composed in German and only later translated into English, for which there was a good and understandable reason. He was namely one of the few German academics who, after leaving their fatherland in the 1930s and then concluding a professional career in America, returned to Germany to spend the remaining years of life. The clever title of the memoir is altogether fitting: ... *immer etwas abseits* (always a bit apart). But the real clue to his self-portrait is a subtle distinction apparent in the subtitle: *Jugenderinnerungen eines jüdischen Berliners*. This is an autobiography written not by a Berlin Jew but by a Jewish Berliner. Tom Angress (as he came to be known to his American friends) spent his first seventeen years fully absorbed by Berlin, and his deep attachment to the city explains much about his trajectory and his eventual return in 1988 to the scene of his youth.[57]

The parents of Werner Angress were typical of many middle-class Jews in Berlin who had worked their way up from humble beginnings to a secure but unpretentious bourgeois social status. As a family they were as integrated as could be, indeed to such an extent that the boy could think of himself as a "German nationalist." However that may be, he was thoroughly Prussian, meaning that he was raised with the strict values of honesty, duty, and frugality – inbred traits that might just as well be ascribed to a Scottish Calvinist. The Angress grandfather lived in Berlin's garment district, not far from Unter den Linden, where he managed a clothing store. He ran a distinctly Jewish household with kosher cuisine and observed the Jewish Sabbath on Friday evenings with a modest candle-lit ceremony ending in a family feast. His son, Werner's father, also presided over a traditional but more secular home of which he was indisputably the authority figure. He was an employee in a private Berlin bank that shriveled during the Great Depression; and he took over the directorship of it when the two owners thereupon disappeared (one, apparently, by suicide). Thus in essence promoted in social rank, the Angress family moved in 1923 to the more fashionable Westend, where Jewish residents were a commonplace. Seldom, nevertheless, was an expression of Yiddish uttered in their apartment. By all appearances, then, this was a rather ordinary middle-class Berlin clan prosperous enough to afford a female servant and a cook.[58]

The mother of Werner Angress was an attractive woman, also a Berlin native, who had grown up beside the Thalia Theater, only a few blocks from the famous downtown department store Kaufhaus des Westens ("KaDeWe" for short), where it still thrives today. Consequently, young Werner was often dragooned into accompanying his mother on her interminable shopping excursions from the Wittenbergplatz along the Tauentzienstrasse, the city's center of female fashion. The boy hated this "consumer madness" of his mother, not to mention her too frequent cuffs on his ear, and he confesses to being "a very moody child" whose relationship with his parents often consequently tended to be chilly and distant.[59]

The one relative who gained Werner's undivided allegiance and affection was his maternal grandfather, Max Kiefer, offspring of a mixed Jewish-Christian family from Upper Silesia who became a fashion designer and who traveled widely from Vienna to Paris and London. Although himself a converted Christian, he married a Jewish girl in Berlin and, reluctantly, reconverted to Judaism. However, he never became a believing or practicing Jew, seldom set foot in a synagogue, and failed to attend the bar mitzvah of Werner Angress or his older brother Fritz.[60]

As for Werner, his recollection was of always being "agnostic" (*areligiös*) and of despising any religious observance that required him to dress up in a jacket and tie. Symptomatic of the Angress family's social integration was their deep prejudice against *Ostjuden*, mostly Hassidim, who around 1900 sought refuge in Berlin from the pogroms of Eastern Europe. Even though these Orthodox Jewish newcomers to Germany lived in another section of the capital and remained largely unseen to Werner Angress, he admittedly shared the antipathy for them felt by his father and grandfather. Apart from Max Kiefer, the other person with whom he maintained an especially warm personal relationship as a boy was a young woman named "Didi," a rather portly (non-Jewish) distant cousin who stayed with the family as a nursemaid for nearly a decade after his birth. Perhaps it was this lack otherwise of a familial closeness that explained his unfortunately chronic and frequent outbursts of temper (*Wutanfälle*) that he struggled to control as a child and later as a man.[61]

The longest and easily the most gripping chapter of the Angress memoir is the one describing his school years. On display in it is an astonishing command of detail – names, places, dates – in part probably because the text was conceived in German and written after the later return to the surroundings of his childhood and not more remotely from America. In the beginning his family had lived near the Bayerischer Platz in the Schöneberg section of Berlin, the "Jewish Switzerland" as it was called because of the many assimilated German Jews there. But the birth of three infant sons in rapid succession created a need for more space and therefore a motive for moving to the Westend. There the Angress family enjoyed the golden years of the Weimar Republic from 1924 to 1932, that is, a period between the Great Inflation and the advent of Nazi dictatorship. It was a relatively luxurious time during which, for instance, the father as bank director was regularly picked up by a chauffeur six days a week and driven to work.[62]

Werner Angress entered an elementary school in 1926. His experience there was totally unproblematic. Most of the pupils, like himself, were from the solid *Mittelstand*, few of them either rich or poor. Although many of his classmates were Jewish, his own best friends were not, and no one thought much of it. In 1930 he shifted for two years to the Herder Realgymnasium, where he never heard an anti-Semitic remark: "friendships between Jewish and non-Jewish youngsters were the rule, not the exception." Angress thus developed the self-image of a normal and reasonably well adjusted pre-teenager, a factor essential to understand his subsequent naïve reaction to Nazism.[63]

When he turned twelve in 1932, barely six months before Hitler's appointment as the German chancellor, young Werner's family moved to Lichterfelde-West, back to a more downscale Berlin. The reasons were largely financial, since the Great Depression had taken a toll. Yet after January 1933 life still went on normally, it seemed, and in fact at Werner's request the family purchased a black-white-red flag (back in vogue after Weimar) and hung it out for Nazi celebrations – a practice stopped by the father after the death of President Paul von Hindenburg in 1934, when Hitler was officially designated as the German Führer.[64] Bowing to his parents' wishes, Werner Angress observed the formality of bar mitzvah at a Wilmersdorf synagogue in December 1933. This appeared almost routine to him, and he attached no religious significance to it. But in richly woven detail he recounts a growing tension thereafter as he began to realize the contradiction between his Jewish heritage and his patriotic enthusiasm. In his new Realgymnasium in the Drakestrasse, near Berlin's Botanic Garden, he at first noticed no difference: "there was never an unfriendly remark, let alone hostility." But in retrospect another reality became much clearer. As he writes in his memoir: "It was the beginning of four more years of gradual isolation, occasional enmity, almost daily small (and later also not so small) humiliations, acts of violence" that were experienced by other Jews, even though the Angress family remained unharmed.[65]

The story of this slow dis-assimilation is told by Angress with a masterful literary touch that recalls the far more famous account by Victor Klemperer. There was a distinct sense of being "different" without an understanding of why. With his blond hair, blue eyes, and compact athletic build Angress certainly did not look the part of a stereotypical Jew propagated in the Nazi press. He did not gesture when speaking, did not have flat feet, and did not reek of garlic. Yet he was a Jew in a school that had only three Jewish pupils, of which the other two were unknown to him. Never an object of derision, he was simply overlooked by his "Aryan" classmates – all the easier, he remarked, because of his short stature. If anything, the situation was a bit tiresome, leading him to speculate that he would not mind belonging to the aristocracy. After all, "Werner von Angress" would not sound bad.[66]

The ill effects of the Nazi takeover were soon enough obvious. Of course, there had been some evidence of German anti-Semitism before 30 January 1933, but for Werner Angress personally things had been "entirely quiet." Now a swastika flew over his apartment building, and at school the "Hitler greeting" was introduced, arms outstretched. He tried to conform, standing with the others at the beginning of each class period to give the Nazi salute and to shout "Heil Hitler." In truth, he did not object to the Führer and on one occasion in the spring of 1934 saw him and Ernst Röhm with some excitement at a public ceremony in Lichterfelde. At the observance of Hindenburg's burial shortly thereafter he joined in singing *Deutschland über alles* and the *Horst-Wessel-Lied* – all quite normal, he felt.[67] Two symptoms of the altered circumstances nonetheless appeared. His school work and consequently his grades began to suffer. In contrast to the preceding Westend years, his Lichterfelde education was "in many ways a fiasco" due to his lagging ambition. Hence the decision for him to leave the Gymnasium without passing the *Abitur* examination, that indispensable ticket to university admission. Meanwhile, he joined one of the Jewish youth organizations (to be sure, the most patriotic among them) and began to devote most of his time to participating in its activities and excursions. In his own mind he was thereby merely joining the ranks of other German youth movements such as the Hitler Jugend and the Bund Deutscher Mädel. He continued to resist his parents' urging to adopt a more Jewish consciousness. Indeed, "at that time I would doubtless have preferred not to be born a Jew."[68]

Why? Inevitably this blunt personal question opens out for the historian onto a broader field of inquiry about the comportment of Germany's Jewish population after 1933. Why did they not leave at once? Why did they remain even after the flagrantly discriminatory Nürnberg Laws of September 1935 and after being stigmatized daily as enemies of the German folk and as racially inferior *Untermenschen*? Like all those who did not escape from Germany until the late 1930s, Angress must face these disturbing issues, and he attempts to respond in personal terms. His initially indulgent attitude toward Nazi rule was not for lack of warning. His father was uncertain and anxious, vaguely hoping at first that "everything will not be eaten as hot as it's cooked." Naturally there was also a fear about forfeiting one's own country and language by plunging into a foreign land. But the father's reservations and criticisms of Hitler's regime mounted after 1935, and he did not hide his concerns from his three sons. Friction in the family grew accordingly, such that Werner's mother scolded him one day for having nothing better to do than defend "those swine up there."[69] Yet the tendencies of public life seemed to him to be tentative and indistinct. He continued to feel pangs of a patriotic spirit whenever brown-shirted columns of SA troopers paraded by with their musical accompaniment. "Moreover, I was convinced that sooner or later the regime would come to a realization of what good Germans we Jews were. And then they would change their stance toward us." In other words, he was a German who happened to be of the Jewish faith, no matter what the Nazis thought.[70] Similar to many assimilated German Jews, he knew much more about Christian than Jewish customs. When very small he had eagerly hunted for Easter eggs in the garden, and he regularly sat under a Christmas tree every December. He had not started attending the Friday Sabbath gatherings of his relatives until the age of nine or ten, doing so only because he enjoyed the candles and the food. No wonder there were for him no thoughts of emigration until he was finally forced to conclude that "Germany does not want me and I do not want the Jews." Many years later he could find his prolonged naïveté regrettable, but at the time it was so.[71]

One event stood out. As mentioned, Angress had joined a Jewish *Bund*, although with the understanding that his organization was but part of a much broader German youth movement and that members of his particular group were only "accidentally" (his word) of the Jewish persuasion. He continued to harbor the hope that their loyalty to the fatherland would finally be appreciated by the Nazi *Obrigkeit* and that they would be eventually integrated into the national cause. They were German "to the core" (*bis in die Knochen*). Alas, this period of secret handshakes, forest hikes, and ski trips was of short duration. The Jewish *Bund* was dissolved. Even though not immediately endangered, Angress suddenly found himself excluded. Only one conclusion could be drawn: "Jews who stressed so much their Germanness, as we did, were unwelcome." Thus, not until after the age of fifteen did he begin to take his father's admonitions seriously. A time was closing that had been marked for him by "youthful romanticism, boyish eroticism, and dubious idealism." However reluctantly, Werner Angress was growing up.[72]

It is clear that he was undergoing one long identity crisis from 1935 to 1937, most of which time he spent at a camp for Jewish adolescents conducted by "Herr Professor" Curt Bondy (actually he held no academic post). This episode in Gross Breesen involved much outdoor activity and intensive vocational training for boys and girls, which turned out to be in purpose and in effect a preparation for emigration. Where? The leading candidates for exile lined up by Bondy were Brazil, Africa, Australia, and the United States. Angress had no idea either of a destination or of a future profession abroad. Decidedly, he preferred to remain in Germany, and when told by his father that the family must leave, he refused. It took Bondy to persuade him to relent.[73] By late October 1937 plans were therefore set, and Angress set off from Berlin on a night train headed for Amsterdam. On the border he was detained and interrogated by the Gestapo. Retrospectively it seemed "a wonder" that he was released and allowed to reach the Netherlands. Yet his feelings remained mixed: Germany was, after all, "the land that despite everything I still incredibly loved." His mother and his two brothers were already safe in London, but the visa problem was unresolved. At loose ends, Angress tarried for weeks in Western Europe: Paris, Reims, Brussels, Bruges, Gent, London, and back to Amsterdam.[74]

Again, it was Curt Bondy who made the difference by telling Angress that he intended to establish a camp like his beloved Gross

Breesen in Virginia. A plea to the American consulate in Rotterdam soon produced a visa – but it would not be valid until 1943! When the European war began with the German invasion of Poland in September 1939, however, it became more urgent to expedite the matter. Finally approved for immigration, Werner Angress thereupon boarded the *SS Veendam* at the end of that October and sailed to the United States. He had definitively left Europe, or had he?[75]

The Atlantic crossing took nearly two weeks in a small vessel badly overcrowded with Jewish refugees. Disappointingly, it landed not in New York harbor but at more pedestrian Hoboken, New Jersey, without a Statue of Liberty. Angress did manage to spend some hours in the big city, strolling through Times Square, drinking the first milk shake of his life, and catching an elevator to the observation deck of the Empire State Building. He was already Tom Angress, having changed his given name while passing through customs from Werner Karl to Werner Thomas. He especially liked the middle initial "T" because it recalled his nickname at Gross Breesen, "Töpper."[76] So it was Tom Angress who traveled on a Greyhound bus to Richmond, Virginia, and soon arrived at nearby Hyde Farmlands to spend the next year and a half planting strawberries, dealing with snakes, and riding horses. For all that, it was not a particularly happy experience on the whole, no second Gross Breesen. His spoken English improved only slowly (always, also as an adult, with a heavy German accent). He missed his family, he continued to suffer from fits of anger and a resulting low self-esteem, and he felt isolated on a tight little island removed from contact with the American way of life. That was suddenly to change. On 7 May 1941 Tom Angress volunteered for the US army.[77]

In uniform he was sent to Fort Meade in Maryland for basic training and then assigned to the Virginia National Guard until the autumn of 1942. For him it was back to a youth movement. But because his naturalization papers were not yet in order, he was denied permission to accompany his unit to Northern Ireland. Instead, he spent some time with an "alien detachment," mostly German Jews, before being transferred to the Military Intelligence Training Center at Camp Ritchie, Maryland, where he was prepped to interrogate German POWs. Meanwhile, unknown to him, his father was arrested in Amsterdam, deported to prison in Berlin, finally herded with other Jews into boxcars heading for Auschwitz, and there murdered in January 1943. At the time Werner T. Angress had never heard the name of Auschwitz and knew nothing of Nazi intentions to carry out a Final Solution. These facts he would not learn until two and a half years later.[78]

In October 1943 Angress at last became an American citizen and was transferred by ship to England, arriving at Liverpool in late January 1944. Initially stationed in a village near Stratford on Avon, he was assigned as an interrogator to an airborne division and sought training as a parachutist, but for undeclared reasons his preparation was delayed. He nonetheless persisted and, after receiving only fifteen minutes of instruction, he jumped from an airplane into German-occupied France on D-Day in May 1944. His narrative account of the ensuing military action is an exciting tale, rich in graphic detail, that would be worthy of a Günter Grass or Norman Mailer. After his plane was struck by anti-aircraft fire, it strayed off course from the initial target of Ste.-Marie l'Église to the French coast near Cherbourg. Landing there alone with his parachute, Staff Sergeant Angress underwent a harrowing escapade that included throwing hand grenades, having his helmet dented by a sniper's bullet, and being wounded by shrapnel. After he had joined a few other straggling American soldiers, they were captured by the Germans. He spent twelve days in captivity, partly at a Cherbourg hospital, until he was released following a German surrender of that entire sector of Normandy to the Allies.[79]

Angress stayed on active duty for eleven months after D-Day. Only a brief span of that time was concerned with his intended function as an interrogator. Incidentally, when asked by POWs why he spoke their language fluently, his standard reply was that he was an American of German descent; he did not reveal either that he was an immigrant or a Jew. His wounds healed, after promotion to the rank of master sergeant, he was thrown back into the fray as the American army was moving closer to the German border. In mid-July 1944 his unit was rotated out of the combat zone and returned to England. Of the 2056 troopers in his regiment who had parachuted on D-Day, 307 were killed and 1161 wounded. Awarded a purple heart and a bronze star, Sergeant Angress had vividly experienced the Second World War, not without sacrifice and not without courage.[80]

There was an ugly aftermath. As the war continued Angress was parachuted once more in September 1944 to the Dutch town of Nijmegen, opposite the German frontier, where he remained until November. This was an Allied defensive position, so his activity there was not strenuous, but it was dangerous. He narrowly averted being killed by an unexploded artillery shell. The so-called Battle of the Bulge in the Ardennes region of Belgium and northern France proved to be the most arduous combat on the Western front. During the two months and two days of that action, between mid-December 1944 and mid-February l945, Sergeant Angress was frequently forced to bivouac outdoors in the cold and snow. Once more, one must search for an apt comparison to his expressive depictions of these scenes. Probably it is fair to say that they most resemble the deft images of battle in the First World War by Erich Maria Remarque or Ernst Jünger.[81]

The end was slow in coming. Once the German military resistance had been seriously weakened, Angress was granted a brief furlough in Paris, time enough for his sexual initiation at the age of twenty-four in a local brothel ("*la première fois?*" she knowingly asked in parting).[82] He was then assigned to the staff of General James Gavin, serving both as chauffeur and interpreter. He also enjoyed two personal encounters with Marlene Dietrich, confirming thereby that she was (among others) Gavin's sometime mistress. Advancing in the meanwhile into Germany, he reached Cologne in April 1945 at a time when the German army still occupied the right bank of the Rhine and the Ruhr. Except for the mighty cathedral, its towers standing though damaged, the city was "a heap of rubble" (*Trümmerhaufen*). Devastation was on all sides, and hence the biting irony of a huge banner hung by the British on the cathedral's façade, a quotation from Adolf Hitler: "Give me four years time and you will not recognize Germany again."[83]

As a part time interrogator Angress had many occasions to talk with German civilians as well as captured soldiers. Most of them were friendly if not fawning, and they were generally glad the war was over for them. They also tended to be highly caustic toward one another, ready with mutual denunciations. Generally they felt defeated rather than liberated. In his diary Angress made an entry about his blunt reaction: "the German nation stinks…. Granted, they are not all criminals, but the great majority is beneath all criticism." By the end of April his unit had reached the Elbe River, where, a few days later, 150,000 German troops surrendered. Therewith the war ended in the field before its official conclusion on 8 May 1945.[84]

The remains of that day were not a pretty sight. Sergeant Angress entered the concentration camp of Wöbbelin to find hundreds of corpses and skeletal humans about. It is striking that he had still never heard of Auschwitz or the Final Solution. Some of the earliest camps for political enemies of the Third Reich were of course known – Dachau, Buchenwald, Sachsenhausen – but ignorance of the exterminations in Eastern Europe remained widespread. Yet now the atrocious reality was becoming apparent, caught forever in the grim newsreel footage that began to circulate. Angress was there as one of those in charge of forcing German civilians and army officers to pass by the open graves.[85]

In mid-May he was given permission by General Gavin to drive a jeep to Amsterdam in search of his family. There he found his mother – frail, weeping, and weighing no more than ninety pounds – as well as his brothers Fritz and Hans (both of whom later emigrated to California). From them he gathered that his father, after a period of incarceration in Germany, had been taken to Auschwitz, which Tom Angress still believed to be, as advertised, merely a work camp. Only much later did he learn the truth. Soon resuming his duties in Germany, he had the possibility of remaining in the force of occupation with the rank of lieutenant. Instead, he longed to return to the United States and to seek an education that would lead him to a profession. Which? By the time he reached Boston harbor in the autumn of 1945, he was still unsure.[86]

In his memoir Tom Angress only sketches the rest of his life – academic career, extensive family, and finally his post-retirement return to Berlin – in a hasty epilogue, under the false assumption that these matters must surely be of little interest to the reader. Modesty misplaced. Still, we can gather a few relevant details. Discharged from the army with the GI Bill in hand, he was admitted to Wesleyan University in Connecticut, where he graduated magna cum laude in 1949. He went on to graduate school at UC Berkeley and received his Ph.D. in 1953. Already married with two sons, as he sighed, his youth was well past. His intellectual interests had quickly shifted at Wesleyan from psychology to history under the influence of Carl Schorske, Sigmund Neumann, and Norman O. Brown. At Berkeley, under Raymond Sontag, he wrote a master's thesis on the Anschluss of Austria in 1938 and a doctoral dissertation about interwar German communism. Like all German migrant scholars of his generation, his personal experience was manifestly crucial in this choice of pursuits. After a brief interlude back at Wesleyan, Angress accepted a temporary appointment in Berkeley's Department of History. As it turned out, he remained there for eight years before acquiring a tenured position at the State University of New York in Stony Brook, where he spent the rest of his academic career, another twenty-five years. Thrice married, he raised two daughters with his American second wife Mili on Long Island while frequently returning to Berlin, before taking up residence there in 1988. Just for the record: three of his four children married non-

Jewish spouses and all of them and their offspring have been raised in a largely secular family atmosphere as non-practicing Jews who observe Christian and well as Jewish holidays.[87]

As for scholarship, the first book by Professor Angress has remained his most important work, entitled *Stillborn Revolution*, published by Princeton University Press in 1963. It is a lucid 500-page analysis of the Communist bid for power in the early Weimar Republic. As the title indicates, this is basically a study of failure, but one that deeply marked Germany's postwar recovery and left a nagging legacy of fear that figured importantly in the reactionary rise of the Nazi Party.[88] After completion of that volume, Angress went on to join a team of scholars connected with the Leo Baeck Institute in New York, a grand research enterprise largely focused on the history of Judaism in Germany to which he contributed a number of penetrating essays.[89] Last but certainly not least appeared his remarkable memoir that recounts the transition of a troubled youth in Berlin to the searing experience of an American soldier thrust into the liberation of his native country from the grip of Nazism. Some immigrant historians from Germany may have enjoyed a more illustrious professional reputation in America, but none led a more turbulent life or portrayed it better.

Chapter Four

PETER GAY

Peter Gay was an only child, and it showed. Born in Berlin in 1923 at the height of the Weimar Republic's runaway inflation, he was not yet ten when the dark wave of National Socialism rolled across his native land. Although too young to have perceived Nazi Germany as an adult, his recollections of youth have a sharp edge and an outspoken anger colorfully expressed. In his memoir, written with his customary dazzling prose style, he admits that he has "derived considerable satisfaction from putting on the record my contempt," not only for the cruelty and callousness of the Nazis but also for those who have ignorantly criticized the assimilated German Jews who hesitated after 1933 to leave the country of their birth and who, as a result, either escaped narrowly from "the German inferno" or would soon perish in it.[90]

All of which gets far ahead of the story of a precocious and often lonely boy, Peter Joachim Fröhlich, who grew up in a lower middle-class family with emotionally restrained parents who made few overt gestures of affection but also never lashed out with a harsh word of criticism. His father was a salesman and junior partner in a modest business firm that supplied porcelain objects and glassware to Berlin department stores and boutiques, with a specialty in wine goblets. He, the father, was from Upper Silesia near Kempen, the son of a hotel proprietor and an autodidact with little formal education. He was slightly plump, did not "look Jewish," and suffered his life long from kidney stones – perhaps not a person from whom one might expect a brilliant progeny.[91] Peter's mother was born in Breslau, where her parents tended a stationery store. She spent most of her early adulthood clerking in her sister's clothing and accessory shop on the Olivaer Platz in Berlin, where they sold goods such as women's underwear, buttons, and thread. She also had her health problems, including a severe onset of tuberculosis in the 1930s that required three wrenching operations. No less troubling, she meanwhile contracted elusive psychosomatic illnesses that were partially inherited by her child. No wonder that the boy, usually looking pale and withdrawn, grew up with a streak of melancholy and with pesky eating disorders. His habitual playmates were two male cousins on his mother's side, about his age, but his faint sketch of them suggests that they were not extremely close. Little Peter Fröhlich was thus often left to his own devices and developed the personality of an unusually "angry" youngster. It followed that his memoir years later should be a story composed with a chip perched squarely on his shoulder about "a poisoning and how I dealt with it."[92]

Peter Fröhlich spent his first thirteen years living in Berlin-Wilmersdorf, a bourgeois area near but not within the much fancier Westend. The family apartments (they moved from one to another) were in the Schweidnitzerstrasse, a side street exactly one block long with a complex of five-story row houses and little traffic. This location was close by the beginning of the prestigious Kurfürstendamm, two miles of shops, bookstores, movie houses, restaurants, and pubs that led to the Gedächtniskirche in downtown western Berlin. If this urban scene was much later to rouse a "silent hatred" in him, Peter as a lad found many reasons to enjoy the city and to praise *"Berliner Luft,"* a reference not only to fresh air but to the wit and mental acuity of the capital's citizenry. In truth, he fit in quite well – until 1933 turned his homeland into an "enduring hell."[93]

From 1929 to 1933 the boy attended an elementary school, of which he retained little memory except a single fistfight. He did recall being thin-skinned und rather humorless, traits attributed to his mother's "neurotic inhibitions," from which "her tensions became mine."[94] The Peter Gay memoir contains several references of that sort, which can surely be ascribed to his later thorough study of Sigmund Freud and to his subsequent psychoanalysis. The result is a tantalizingly introspective self-evaluation that nonetheless refrains from unduly intimate revelations about the family. On the surface, at least, things seemed to be unfolding well enough. At age nine he moved on to the Goethe Realschule, his admission assured by the fact that his father was a wounded veteran of the First World War and proud bearer of an Iron Cross. This new school was sober and non-political: "I was never ridiculed, never harassed, never attacked." He did not feel at all disadvantaged by his teachers because of being Jewish, and he was not forced to sing Nazi anthems like the *Horst-Wessel-Lied*. An open question remains whether this was altogether typical of German schools before 1945.[95]

The political sensation of 30 January 1933 made little impression on the pre-teen Peter Fröhlich. But the Reichstag fire a month later did, notably because his father expressed strong doubts that the deed had been done solely by a demented Dutchman named Van der Lubbe, as the Nazis claimed. A positive attitude was still possible when the parliamentary elections early that March brought the Nazi Party only 44 percent of the popular vote. That outcome did not prevent passage of the Enabling Act a fortnight later nor the beginning of a boycott on Jewish doctors, lawyers, and retail stores in Berlin (*"Kauft nicht bei Juden"*). Sensitive to slights, Peter began to notice personal effects at school as well, and the memoir expresses his lingering hatred – that is the word – for a blond classmate named Hans Schmitt, a bully who joined the Hitler Jugend and who delighted in spreading anti-Semitic slogans: "May his bones lie rotting in Russian soil."[96]

There were other obvious symptoms of change for the family, such as losing their non-Jewish servant Johanna after proclamation of the Nürnberg Laws in 1935. Yet, paradoxically, the father's business was thriving amid a general economic recovery, enabling the Fröhlichs to move to a larger apartment in the Sächsische Strasse, still in Wilmersdorf but farther downtown, just off of the Kurfürstendamm. They also enjoyed a memorable auto tour in 1936: Wittenberg, Leipzig, Weimar, Frankfurt, Koblenz, plus the Rhine and Moselle valleys.[97]

In hindsight another reality was irrepressible: "We had suddenly become Jews." Before 1933 the family tradition was not simply irreligious but antireligious. Certainly, the parents had some Jewish friends and relatives, but they consciously rejected any tribal affiliation. "They were Germans." Although they occasionally employed Yiddish expressions, as did many Germans, they carefully avoided the term *goy* to designate an "Aryan," another forbidden word. Little Peter was circumcised, but it remained unclear whether this represented Jewish ritual or medical procedure. At the same time, the Fröhlichs evinced no inclination to join the Christian faith, as many Jews had done to seal their assimilation. It was therefore fitting for a strong-willed atheist that, in the 1950s, the father's funeral was not conducted by a rabbi.[98]

What of a bar mitzvah for the son? "I pleaded ignorance, indifference, even hostility: the Jewish religion meant nothing to me." But it was 1935, the year of the Nürnberg Laws, and Peter was susceptible to the argument that he should display solidarity with an increasingly oppressed minority. In the end, however, he declined and his parents were not ones to insist.[99] He did consent to join the *Ringbund*, a kind of Jewish Boy Scout troop, but only so that he could join in hiking and camping as part of the larger German youth movement of the 1930s. If the boy had any religion it was soccer. Although rather unathletic himself, he was passionately devoted to his hometown team of Hertha B.S.C. and often rooted for them in Berlin's giant Olympic Stadium.[100]

The predictable outcome in the case of Peter Fröhlich was a child deeply troubled by the crosscurrents and ambiguities during the first decade of Nazi rule. On one hand he was adept at developing strategies of survival, for instance stamp collecting – particularly those marvelous 1923 issues from the Great Inflation of the Weimar Republic when the original values were printed over with sums of the billions and trillions. And especially sports, including the

Olympic games of 1936, when he cheered lustily for Jesse Owens and the American squad. He records that the high point of his youth was a great soccer match between England and Germany in May 1938 attended by a crowd of a hundred thousand spectators in the Olympic Stadium (won by the English, he recalled, 6-3).[101] Such events stirred strong emotions in him and served to create an illusion of normalcy. Yet meanwhile there was constantly the loud contrary drumbeat of background events that could not be shut out: "the anti-Semitic campaigns, calculated to drive us to despair, were so incessant, so repetitious, so all-embracing that it was nearly impossible to escape them." How to square the circle? Some Jews, of course, continued to believe that an accommodation with Hitler's regime was feasible. Such optimism was decidedly not shared by Peter's father nor, accordingly, by him. For them the current legislation and propaganda were no more than a pack of lies, totally "unhistorical and unscientific." As a consequence, grudgingly, they began to contemplate emigration. Most likely it would be to the United States, where they fortunately had wealthy relatives living in Florida, an Uncle Alfred who had married an American girl, Aunt Grace, and taken up residence there.[102]

As this story slowly unravels, it unavoidably raises the insoluble conundrum in any memoir of separating actual experiences from later recollections of them. A certain skepticism is in order. It seems fair to tax the older Peter Gay, looking back at his youth, with embellishing the tale with premonitions, that is, ascribing greater awareness and stronger convictions to a lad of ten than he was likely to have had. Such was his age at the time of the Nazi seizure of power, and he had barely reached his teens when the Fröhlich family left Germany. To register that caveat here is only to underscore his undoubtedly accurate impression that the road to Auschwitz "was never straight nor foreseeable." For assimilated German Jews the situation was drenched with ambiguity, and Gay is surely justified to chastise those self-anointed critics who ex post facto lament that Germany Jewry was not quick enough to respond to the advent of tyranny and to depart at once. He forcefully reminds us that even the Nazi power brokers had no clear conception by 1937 of what their policy toward the Jews was to be and that the Final Solution was not yet formulated or promulgated as an immutable political doctrine. Of course there were questions – open questions – about what the future held, but generally those critics have little bothered to understand the dilemma faced by a family like the Fröhlichs before 1939.[103]

The testimony of Peter Gay's memoir is that he first realized that "the road ahead would be hard" and that it was "high time to act" at the age of thirteen in May 1937 while listening to a mocking radio speech by Joseph Goebbels. The trigger for action was a visit by Uncle Alfred and Aunt Grace from Florida. As the Nazi noose tightened, a plan was devised: first Peter's elder cousin Hanns would be sent abroad, then himself and the younger cousin Edgar, finally the parents and another uncle (with the ultra-Germanic name Siegfried). By the summer of 1938, in the wake of Austria's Anschluss, little else mattered than escape. "But who would have us?"[104] Peter was already expelled from his school, and his father had been forced out of a job by his non-Jewish senior partner. Even though the father possessed no special skill and not the trace of a foreign language, they would need to leave Germany. Applications were hastily submitted for residence in Great Britain as in the meantime events approached a climax. The fateful agreement – not to say Anglo-French capitulation – at Munich in September 1938 was followed by the literally shattering experience of *Kristallnacht* on 10 November. As he pedaled his tiny bicycle in the Tauentzienstrasse that evening through shards of broken glass from store windows, Peter Fröhlich saw at first hand "the German nightmare." Now there could no longer be any doubt about leaving.[105]

Because of the strict quota limitations for American visas, the family's first hope was England. But there was a serious complication. Since the father was born in a fringe area of Silesia lost to Poland after the First World War, he counted as a Pole, not a German. Hence the Fröhlichs were turned down by the Home Office for admission to Britain in December 1938, causing the child Peter to sink into a slough of depression. What to do? Curiously, Shanghai was a possibility, but it was the New World they wanted to reach, and time was pressing. On 15 March 1939 the German army moved in to occupy what remained of Czechoslovakia. A few weeks later, on 21 April, a passport was finally issued to Peter Israel Fröhlich. The new middle name was of course a gift from Adolf Hitler, along with a large red "J" for *Jude*.[106] He was free to leave with his parents if only arrangements for their exile could be made. The solution was Cuba. Reservations were obtained on the Hapag steamship *St. Louis* that was to leave from Hamburg to Havana on 13 May. But they then learned of the possibility to depart on another Hapag liner *Iberia* on 27 April, a fortnight sooner. In this instance, details mattered. The advance of date may appear slight, but it turned out to make every difference. The final formalities of departure were Peter Fröhlich's last contact with brown-shirted officials. He behaved properly, but his regained composure "never stopped me from hating the guts of the swine who were lording over us."[107] With that touching sentiment the family caught a train to Hamburg, climbed aboard the *Iberia*, and enjoyed a brief farewell tour of European ports: Antwerp, Southampton, Cherbourg, and Lisbon. They arrived in Havana on 13 May 1939, less than three and a half months before the German invasion of Poland touched off the Second World War. Free at last, and free at the very last minute.[108]

The elder historian Peter Gay, reliving these distant events in his memoir, would have to count himself among the lucky few whose immediate family escaped without bodily harm. They were luckier than they then realized, since the *St. Louis*, for which their original reservations had been secured, was turned back from Havana when it attempted to dock there on 27 May, nor was it permitted to unload its passengers at an American port. After returning to Europe, the ship was allowed to deposit about a third of them in Britain; the rest arrived back on the Continent to face an unknown and potentially disastrous fate. At age fifteen Peter Gay, as he would henceforth call himself, had thereby turned his back on his birthplace, which nonetheless remained deep in his consciousness: "fragments of Nazi Berlin still sometimes haunt me and will haunt me to the day I die."[109]

The sojourn in Cuba was clearly a temporary respite, during which Gay improved his English and prepared for a life in the United States. In addition to the relatives in Florida, another aunt and uncle meanwhile reached Atlanta, where they opened a store and a home with room for their nephew. Accordingly, he left Havana and arrived at Key West in January 1941, whence he reached Atlanta and finally joined his parents in Denver, Colorado, at the foot of the Rocky Mountains. There in the American Middle West he was admitted to high school as a senior and graduated in the next year before entering Denver University with a full scholarship at the age of twenty. Bright and adaptable, with an impeccable academic record, he was becoming indistinguishably American. Yet he could not altogether shake off lasting effects of "the Nazi poison" in his system — a metaphor used repeatedly throughout his memoir. He saw the war from afar, but his "hatred" for Germany and Germans remained at a "high pitch." He welcomed news of the bombing of Hamburg and Cologne and did not blanch at reports about the destruction of Dresden or Berlin. They only fed his "imperious hankering for revenge." Few migrants from Germany could muster as much contempt as Peter Gay.[110]

Appropriately, he could not later consider himself a survivor of the Holocaust. He had neither been incarcerated nor engaged in any military action. Instead, he spent the balance of the war peacefully as a college student in Denver and earned his BA there just as it was ending in 1945. He entered graduate school at Columbia University in New York at the age of twenty-three in September 1946. Very slowly thereafter, "subtly and invisibly," his reconciliation with Germany began through his historical studies. His doctoral dissertation was devoted to the revisionist leader of German Social Democracy before the First World War, Eduard Bernstein, which became his first book in 1952.[111] Indicatively, research for this topic could be conducted in Amsterdam at the International Institute for Social History, where the Bernstein papers are located, not in Germany. Gay could easily have visited the postwar *Bundesrepublik* during this time but chose not to do so. Yet he was beginning, as he awkwardly put it, to "rethink my feelings" and to "unfreeze" somewhat. With his wife Ruth he rather tensely crossed the bridge between Strasbourg and Kehl in June 1961, nearly twenty-two years after leaving German soil (and, as it happened, only weeks before the hasty construction of the Berlin Wall). Invited to lecture at Berlin's Free University in Dahlem, Gay took the occasion to visit the sites where little Peter Fröhlich had ridden his bike. He had to confess that he was perturbed at first whenever he heard German spoken in the street, as if pollution of the language during the Third Reich had never occurred. And he recounts an incident that well summed up the source of his unease. While changing money at a kiosk near the border in Baden, he believed that he detected an anti-Semitic disdain in the indifferent gaze of a female official. But "the fact was that this clerk did not hate me; she barely registered my existence. I hated her."[112] All in all, Berlin was a letdown, no longer the city of his boyhood, still marked as it was by scarred buildings and neglected ruins. When walking through his old neighborhood, past his elementary school and Gymnasium, he felt little emotion and certainly no nostalgia. He was not moved even by viewing the damaged remains of the Gedächtniskirche: was it a condemnation of Nazism or a criticism of Allied bombing? Otherwise the architecture of rebuilt postwar structures appeared all too functional and uninspiring. This negative reaction was surely yet another indication that his "silent hatred" for all things German was scarcely attenuated.[113]

Still struggling with these residual emotions, Peter Gay was in the meanwhile launching his exceptional scholarly career in the

United States. Now a professor at Columbia, he was invited for an academic year, 1963-1964, to the Center for Advanced Study in the Behavioral Sciences near the Stanford campus in Palo Alto, California. In addition to publishing a volume of essays on the French Enlightenment, he began a two-volume survey of the European Enlightenment – including the German *Aufklärung* – and also started a third project that culminated in the publication of his acclaimed book about *Weimar Culture* in 1968.[114] The latter was undoubtedly influenced by his acquaintance during the Stanford year with Karl Dietrich Bracher, a world-famous political scientist, author of a massive study of the demise of the Weimar Republic, and a relative by marriage of the famous hero of the German Resistance Dietrich Bonhoeffer. More significantly, perhaps, Gay's relationship with the Bracher family helped him to break out of his "fixed pattern of response to my native land." Admittedly he was still not "disposed to forgive those who did not deserve forgiveness." Yet, after another few years, he did return to Berlin to spend several months there and felt himself "more or less" at home again. More or less.[115]

At least he proved to be far less inhibited in his research and writing as he went on to undertake extensive studies of Freudian psychology and, in the years between 1984 and 1998, to produce an astonishing total of five volumes in a gigantic examination of the late nineteenth-century European bourgeoisie. In the course of these prolific labors, in his own judgment, he had at last "managed largely to free myself from the poisons of my past." Maybe so, but the reader of his memoir cannot fail to observe that, conspicuously, the qualifying adverb "largely" still obtains.[116]

As a concluding afterthought, the author asks himself whether he has remained a Berliner. Certainly not in the same sense that he was when there as a boy in the 1930s. True, Peter Fröhlich is long gone, but part of him has lived on in Peter Gay.

Chapter Five

FRITZ STERN

The autobiography by Fritz Stern, well over 500 pages in all, deserves to be called just that. It is not merely a memoir of his personal experience during one significant phase of his life, but a full-length summary of German history after 1871 and of his own participation in it. Born in 1926, he knew the German Empire at first hand not at all, the Weimar Republic as a very small boy, and the Third Reich only for five years before reaching teenage. Leaving Germany at the age of twelve to settle in the United States, he essentially grew up as an American of German descent, and as an adult he adopted a thoroughly American view of Europe. The five Germanys of which he writes were thus known to him from afar, despite frequent visits to the land of his origin, and his account of them both gains and loses value because of this distanced perspective.[117]

The Stern family was centered in the Silesian capital of Breslau (now Polish Wroclaw), which, after its annexation to Germany in 1871, became the second largest city in Prussia. Breslau was thus no provincial backwater but a bustling commercial metropolis on the Oder River that quadrupled in size during the five decades before 1910. Its population was nearly sixty percent Protestant, a third Catholic, and only five percent Jewish (about 20,000). But this demographic profile had one striking anomaly: almost half of Breslau's physicians were Jews. Hence the most significant fact about Fritz Stern's forebears was that his four great-grandfathers, both his grandfathers, and his father were all MDs. They were, in other words, perfect representatives of the German *Bildungsbürgertum*, that new late nineteenth-century educated and well-to-do middle class of citizens. Many among them, dating back at least two generations, were converts from Judaism to Christianity, so that Fritz Stern's infant baptism as a Lutheran Protestant was a matter taken for granted by the family.[118]

In Stern's account, his own persona thus fitted comfortably into circumstances of the rise of German Jewry, "one of the most spectacular social leaps in European history." People like him were closely attached to German culture; they were "genuinely at home." Such status by no means precluded awareness of a Jewish background – indeed, he wrote, "Jewishness posed the deepest quandaries" – yet that remained a subliminal topic usually not discussed. Like most Breslau Jews of their social station, the Sterns had long before lost any trace of Yiddish, and they spoke *Hochdeutsch* at home. This was especially appropriate since the two grandfathers, Oskar Briege and Richard Stern, both became university professors of medicine and led "comfortable, respected lives."[119] Fritz Stern's father Rudolf had a rockier career path after he joined the German army in 1914, was wounded and awarded the Iron Cross (second and first class), and thus began his studies somewhat belatedly. But he, too, became a noted Breslau physician, an expert in forensic medicine and author of a reputable book on that subject. To this may be added that Rudolf's wife Käthe, Fritz's mother, earned a doctorate in physics. All in all, then, the German Kaiserreich to which Fritz Stern later devoted most of his scholarly research was a period of notable academic achievement and thoroughgoing assimilation for his family.[120]

In the immediate postwar years after 1918 Rudolf and Käthe were married, first in a civil ceremony, then in a Lutheran church with a text from St. John, and they promptly begot three children: Fritz Stern and his two sisters. The father served briefly in Berlin at the behest of a famous family friend, Fritz Haber, a 1920 Nobel laureate in chemistry. But after the onset of hyperinflation in 1923, the young family soon returned to Breslau, where Fritz was born three years later. In the autobiography he claims that his earliest recollections were of the Weimar Republic's glowing years in the later 1920s, but he was all of three years old when the economic crash of 1929 occurred. Despite that, his own family continued to prosper well enough, thanks to the father's appointment in the medical school at the University of Breslau. They consequently moved from the Kaiser Wilhelm Strasse into a seven-room apartment in a more affluent downtown area of the city, which provided housing for the family and space for Dr. Stern's medical practice. They could also afford vacations in the Engadine Valley, just south of St.-Moritz in Switzerland, at a village adjacent to Sils Maria, later to become Fritz Stern's "elective home" in Europe. From this point on, the early 1930s, Stern's childhood memories become much sharper, although one must wonder about the remark that he was (at age four or five) "reading about Napoleon at the time."[121]

The years prior to 1933 gave unavoidable evidence of change. In Breslau the Nazi Party climbed from a popular vote of one percent in 1928 to 24 percent in 1930. In July 1932 that figure rose to 37 percent nationwide, and there was irrepressible violence in the streets. As a youngster Fritz Stern quickly learned to avoid uniformed SA troopers marching and singing in downtown Breslau. In November 1932 the national suffrage of the Nazis dropped to 33 percent, but in Breslau it held at nearly seven points higher.[122] Nonetheless, little Fritz could still lead a "sheltered" existence while he entered a private boy's school in April 1932. Not yet seven years old, as he recounts, "I was on the way to becoming a spoiled and hence unhappy child, enveloped in comfortable privilege and parental adulation." He must have had some political awareness, since, on his way from school on 30 January 1933, he picked up a single-page newspaper extra with a headline that Adolf Hitler was the German chancellor and took it home to his father. Yet there is no need to exaggerate. It seems fitting, rather, that Stern's retrospective narrative of Weimar's final moments twice employs the telling phrase: "I caught a glimpse," that is, a child's-eye view of his first Germany.[123]

Germany's submission to the Nazi regime proceeded unhindered, it seemed, and the slowly accelerating disaggregation of Jews began at a time when no one yet realized the full implications of what was happening. After the Enabling Act and the so-called Day of Potsdam, when Hitler in effect received the blessing of President von Hindenburg, the purge of Jewish civil servants and professional men commenced – meaning, among others, university professors and hospital physicians, people like the Sterns. Moreover, fear settled in like a fog, prompted by news of the Dachau concentration camp and the rasping voice of the Führer on radio. Fritz Stern's residual condemnation of the German nation was categorical: "Never before had a modern, educated, proudly civilized class so readily abandoned, betrayed, and traduced the most basic rights of citizens."[124] Meantime, relatively soon, his parents realized the danger and determined to seek emigration. They used a vacation trip to Italy to scout out possibilities there and elsewhere. The father, ceasing his lecturing but maintaining his private medical practice, contacted one of his sisters living in France and through her obtained a temporary position at a hospital in Paris, which he hoped would lead to a secure post in Tunisia. In the company of his father, Fritz Stern traveled in an overnight train via Berlin to Paris. As they passed by Brussels, he relates, the two of them broke out lustily singing *"La Marseillaise"* and *"L'Internationale"* (Fritz in French at age seven?). They camped out with relatives in Neuilly for a brief while, but Tunisia faded as a possible refuge and the stay in Paris proved temporary. However, they were still in the French capital on 6 February 1934, the date of street riots near the Place de la Concorde, directly across the Seine from the National Assembly building. The sight of public tumult and overturned vehicles left a "vivid impression." Shortly thereafter, they returned to Breslau.[125]

For the first time Fritz Stern began to reflect seriously about his German and Jewish identity. Remarkably, he records that before 1933 "I didn't even know about my Jewish roots." He was brought up short one day when, after he used an anti-Semitic epithet during an argument with his sister, he was firmly reproved and enlightened by his father. This led, not uncommonly, to a kind of identity crisis: since he was not fully Christian nor fully Jewish, and henceforth certainly not a pure "Aryan," was he any longer German? Like so many converted Jews, he had known only Christian traditions since early childhood. He gladly joined in Easter and Christmas festivities, he read the New Testament as well as the Old, and he said his prayers every evening before bedtime. Yet back in school, after entering the Maria Magdalena Gymnasium in 1936, he was suddenly confronted with verbal and once physical abuse on the playground. These rare incidents were enough to cause the boy to withdraw emotionally into his family: "I lived prematurely on the edge of an adult world."[126]

Whether it was literally true or not of the Stern family that "spiritually we already lived in exile," the parents were certainly preoccupied by the thought of emigration, especially after proclamation of the Nürnberg Laws in 1935. Their attention now turned to the United States, though it was far away and the father preserved hopes to find a place to practice medicine within or nearer Europe. Pisa or Ankara? Apart from the distressing uncertainties of such a total displacement, "it was hard enough to resolve leaving your home, your language, your German past."[127] So life in Breslau continued for a while longer, alternating between feelings of normalcy and estrangement. But attendance at Maria Magdalena became "increasingly unpleasant" for the boy, surrounded at times by uniforms of the Hitler Jugend and forced to listen to Nazi anthems, in which he did not join; nor did he yell "*Heil Hitler*" like the others. Finally, he was the lone "non-Aryan" at his school and felt totally isolated, "not knowing when or from where the next insult would come." In short, his was a familiar Jewish story of gradual social erosion. One scene poignantly expressed Fritz Stern's growing frustration. In 1936 the Stern family traveled for a long weekend to Prague, where they sought out a Jewish cemetery. Before leaving, as was customary, little Fritz left a written wish under a pebble atop a tombstone. It read: "give us a chance to escape our dreadful country."[128]

Once back at "my hated school," Stern developed a plan for his family to establish an exile in Prague. Alerting his parents to this fantasy (not long before the dismemberment of Czechoslovakia!) led to no action, but it may have prodded them into more urgent consideration of a move to the United States. They briefly visited there in April 1938 and then returned to Breslau again to address the necessary formalities of emigration.[129] Meanwhile, events were beginning to overtake them as Austria was absorbed *"Heim ins Reich."* In relating these developments of the late 1930s, Stern raises the inevitable and most disturbing question posed by others: why did they wait so long to leave Germany? Not alone, they feared abandoning the only homeland they knew in order to face the perplexities of a strange country in a foreign language. But it was by now patent that they had "no future in Germany whatsoever."[130] Ultimately, not before mid- September 1938, the Sterns were able to obtain visas at the American Embassy in Berlin (Fritz was number 757) and to book passage on the *SS Statendam* for the last day of that month. As their overnight train left Breslau for the final time, the son felt "nothing but joy." His father wept. In the German capital, Fritz's Aunt Lotte saw them off at the Tempelhof airport, whence they flew to Schiphol near Amsterdam, then moved on to England. They returned to Holland just in time to catch their ship at

Rotterdam on the same day that the Munich conference surrendered the Sudetenland to Nazi Germany. Fritz Stern knew no English and had no notion of America other than the cowboy stories of Karl May, but he was overcome with "joyous relief and wondrous excitement."[131]

When entering New York harbor, Fritz Stern recalls, "I think I caught a glimpse of the Statue of Liberty through a porthole." Another glimpse? It is improbable, since his ship landed in Hoboken, New Jersey. In any event his destination was not Manhattan but a crowded apartment in Queens where, not yet thirteen, he was entered into Public School 152. Almost immediately news arrived of *Kristallnacht*. "Such a narrow escape!" Had they left six weeks later and it could have happened to the Sterns. If his father had been taken away, incarcerated and abused or worse, "it would have poisoned me forever against all things German."[132] That did not occur, and the remainder of Stern's autobiography reveals how he grew up as an American and came to view, even to appreciate, Germany through American eyes. The family adapted with alacrity. His father studied assiduously to pass an examination for a medical license and succeeded after only two months, thereupon opening an office in Manhattan. Fritz's older sister Toni was admitted to Bryn Mawr College. Although the family still spoke German at home, the boy was adeptly learning English at school and earned his spending money by delivering groceries for a local Queens market. He hardly felt handicapped, although he proved to be "distressingly shy with girls," perhaps not as unusual as he imagined.[133]

Initially the Sterns kept up some contacts by mail with Europe, but the news from there went from bad to worse. After conclusion of the Nazi-Soviet pact in 1939, the German *Wehrmacht* invaded Poland, later Norway, and then in May 1940 France and the Lowlands. On the day that German troops marched down the Champs-Élysées in Paris, Fritz Stern stayed home from school. Correspondence with Europe dwindled and after Pearl Harbor ceased altogether. Only belatedly was it learned that one European aunt had committed suicide, while another with her husband was sent to Auschwitz, their tragic end station. At the time, as was generally the case, the existence of concentration camps was known to him, Stern remembered, but not the gas chambers.[134]

Fritz Stern entered Bentley High School in Manhattan on a scholarship and manifestly did very well there, even becoming editor of the school newspaper, a testimony to his improved English skills. After skipping the sophomore year, he graduated in June 1943 and immediately thereupon enrolled at Columbia College, where he found Allen Ginsberg as a close friend and Jacques Barzun and Lionel Trilling as teachers. These names suggest a reason why, instead of medicine, his interests turned to history and literature.[135] His response to reports from Germany was indicative of his progressive Americanization. He felt little compassion for victims of the fire bombings in Hamburg and Dresden. Furthermore, he was entirely skeptical about the ulterior motives of the conspirators in the plot against Hitler on 20 July 1944, considering that they were "merely old-style Junkers or Prussian officers following their own nationalistic interests." No wonder, then, that Germany's unconditional surrender was greeted by Stern with "relief ... mixed with hatred."[136]

In the first postwar years Fritz Stern became a US citizen, husband, father, and university professor. It was symptomatic enough that his first wife Peggy Bassett was a New England Puritan and that his two children Fred and Katherine were not brought up bilingually. He had no direct contacts with a still politically amorphous Germany, though his historical focus noticeably shifted in that direction under the aegis of Professor Henry Roberts, a student of the exiled Hajo Holborn at Yale and a former army intelligence officer through whom Stern joined a coterie that included OSS veterans like H. Stuart Hughes, Leonard Krieger, Carl Schorske, Franz Neumann, and Felix Gilbert. Another acquaintance was Chaim Weizmann, who piqued his interest in Israel. If faintly pro-Zionist in his fashion, Stern remained "totally secular" and nominally Christian, disinclined as he was to convert to Judaism. To be sure, Adolf Hitler had made him a Jew, though against his will. Hence the defiant tone of "I am an American and a Jew."[137]

Stern's chapter on the West German Federal Republic, founded in 1949, is the longest of his autobiography and the heart of the book. He was initially "deeply distrustful" of the *Bundesrepublik* without realizing that it would come to have a great impact on his life, "which was still marked by deep repugnance for almost all things German."[138] At first he longed to return to Europe, but not to Germany, and he was one of those who would not dream of purchasing a German automobile. Yet he was meanwhile beginning to teach German history and to complete research on his Ph.D. dissertation topic: the precursors of Nazism in Wilhelmine and Weimar Germany. For obvious reasons he was fascinated by the study of what he called the "German ideology," which was anti-modern, anti-West, anti-Liberal, and often anti-Semitic.[139] His first return to Europe was not until 1950, when he toured England, revisited Paris, and entered very briefly into Germany. Like all those American immigrants who had seen something of the 1930s, he was seriously disturbed by encountering German uniforms again, "but perhaps I was superimposing Nazi faces on which might have been innocent people."[140] A longer European expedition was made possible by a Ford faculty exchange program in 1954, during which the Stern family resided for several weeks in Berlin-Dahlem, the city's "Little America." Fritz Stern had never lived in Berlin before (as a child, he said, he was better acquainted with London and Paris), and he found much to explore in the now divided German capital. Although he had second thoughts on his earlier judgment about Claus Schenk von Stauffenberg and Hitler's other would-be assassins, he could not overcome his suspicions of Germany's fledgling democracy, and above all he abhorred the self-pity too often evident in random conversations with Germans. As for the uniformed *Volkspolizei* in East Berlin, they effortlessly increased his "unease."[141]

Crucial in three regards was an academic year, 1957-1958, spent at the Center for Advanced Study in the Behavioral Sciences near Stanford. First, it gave Stern time to revise his doctoral dissertation, which appeared in 1961 as *The Politics of Cultural Despair*, a study of three German thinkers – Paul de Lagarde, Julius Langbehn, and Arthur Moeller van den Bruck – who easily qualified in his analysis as proto-Nazis. Never one to stint on deserved praise of his performance, Stern found it "gratifying that the book was well received and has remained in print."[142] Second, Stern became a constant friend of another fellow at the CASBS, the brilliant German sociologist Ralf Dahrendorf. It was through this bond that his persistently negative attitude toward Germany began to evolve in a more benevolent direction. He was not alone to discover in one decent and humane person a good reason to hope for postwar Germany's rehabilitation.[143] Third, and most important as it turned out, was Stern's close association with the economic historian David Landes. The partnership developed (and later dissolved) through this connection led Fritz Stern to the signature project of his academic career, a biography of Gerson Bleichröder, Bismarck's personal and official banker in Berlin. Apart from its inherent significance for the history of the Second Reich, this research could be viewed as the gateway to a more expansive topic that was to occupy Stern and many other scholars for years to come: the twisted relationship of Germans and Jews. In pursuit of this grail, Stern accepted an SSRC grant for 1960-1961 to plumb the Rothschild archives in Paris as well as Bismarck's family collection at the Chancellor's post-1871 estate at Friedrichsruh near Hamburg.[144]

Following that satisfying year in Europe, Stern began to set his foot on the path to celebrity. Invited to the Kennedy White House by Arthur Schlesinger, Jr., he presented there a report on contemporary Germany that, in printed form, made a splash in the prestigious journal *Foreign Affairs*, to which he contributed numerous other articles and book reviews thereafter. He became active in the presidential Council on Foreign Relations and also participated as an American representative at Braunschweig's International Institute for Textbook Research that addressed the tangled problem of unifying various national interpretations of recent history in European schools.[145] His conspicuous involvement at the intersection of scholarship and politics prompted, in turn, an invitation in 1964 to join in a panel at Berlin's Free University, where two lions of the German historical profession, Fritz Fischer and Gerhard Ritter, faced off in a heated debate on the issue of German imperialism before and during the First World War. While recognizing some exaggeration in Fischer's blockbuster book, *Griff nach der Weltmacht*, Stern essentially sided with his interpretation. That statement was subsequently published, without his expressed consent, in the weekly *Der Spiegel*, further fanning an already roiling controversy reaching well beyond the university campus. "It was a heady experience."[146]

The year 1966-1967 was devoted to a sabbatical at Oxford, where Stern kept company with the British luminaries James Joll and Alan Bullock. The Bleichröder volume was still uncompleted, and it became more so when a tip from Hans-Ulrich Wehler caused him to return to Friedrichsruh to uncover further documentary stashes of Bismarck's correspondence. These were to provide an "indispensable substructure" for his manuscript that continued to grow in complexity.[147] In the midst of this string of successes abroad, Stern regularly held down his teaching position at Columbia and became irresistibly embroiled in the anti-Vietnam War demonstrations there in the late 1960s. While no rabid partisan of the war party, he could not suppress his apprehensions about those self-appointed gurus – prominent among them Herbert Marcuse – whose influence was stirring such mass student radicalism that it apparently threatened to destroy the university. The worst of those elements, in Stern's view, were all too reminiscent of the SA storm troopers who had tramped through the streets of Breslau thirty years before.[148]

After the withdrawal of David Landes from the Bleichröder project, Fritz Stern soldiered on during summers at his cabin in Vermont and between his increasingly frequent forays to Europe.

He also acquired a small home in Princeton, nearby the Institute for Advanced Study, an ideal location to hobnob on weekends with distinguished fellows such as Felix Gilbert, Karl Dietrich Bracher, Thomas Nipperdey, Hans-Ulrich Wehler and Jürgen Kocka, Hans and Wolfgang Mommsen. This roster of academic personalities was augmented by political dignitaries like Helmut Schmidt and Helmut Kohl. While sharing a platform with the loquacious Chancellor Schmidt, Stern was awarded the Officers' Cross of West German Order of Merit, just one of his many postwar trophies.[149]

In 1976, after sixteen years of intermittent labor, Fritz Stern finally completed a draft of his Bismarck-and-Bleichröder saga, published in February of the year following. As a rule the reviewers were "extremely kind" and indeed "generous," he took note, although a few regarded his work as an unoriginal and old-fashioned example of the biographical genre. Apart from scholarly debates raised by the book, it left one fundamental question unresolved. In the larger and more conventional opening section Stern presented a convincing portrait of Bleichröder's special relationship with Bismarck, made possible because there had been no main affiliate of the Rothschild banking dynasty in Berlin. But in the concluding portion of the study Stern attempted to portray Bleichröder as a quintessential representative of the newly emerging middle class of German businessmen in the late nineteenth century. How could he, the first ennobled German Jew and certainly the most outstanding of his era, be both unique and typical? Stern's volume, although otherwise deeply researched and gorgeously written, offered no solution for this contradiction.[150]

After the Weimar and Nazi periods, plus the postwar Bonn Republic, Fritz Stern's fourth Germany was the East German regime, known to everyone in town by its Teutonic initials as the DDR. Here he seems a bit out of his element, as were most westerners when they peered across the Berlin Wall. Admittedly, Stern's direct personal contacts there were "minimal," and he thus observed life in the DDR only "from afar." Yet on occasional visits the sight of cobblestone streets and shabby store fronts reminded him of Germany of bygone days, and he enigmatically commented: "I felt bizarrely at home there precisely because I wasn't." While teaching at the Free University in West Berlin in the summer of 1954, still well before the Wall was built, he crossed over to the eastern sector to attend theater and to browse in the Karl Marx bookstore on the Stalinallee. Thereafter he had no further contact for several years until the sabbatical year 1961-1962, when personal acquaintances in Paris netted him a visa to tour East Germany. He visited Merseburg and there sniffed oppressive brown coal dust from the Leuna chemical works, as well as Naumburg's illustrious Gothic cathedral, and Schulpforta where Leopold von Ranke and Friedrich Nietzsche counted among the alumni. Poking into the archives of Potsdam, he befriended Dr. Stefan Brather, one of the head archivists, who accompanied him on an excursion to the nearby park and castle of Sans Souci. Stern seemed unaware of the risk being taken through his cordiality by Brather, who was later interrogated by the Stasi and dismissed from his post for having unduly close relations with a number of Western scholars. Stern does confess that his "greatest failure" was an underestimation of the Stasi during the DDR years. After the early 1960s he conducted no more research in East Germany, though whenever in Berlin he did venture beyond the Wall "with some regularity." The conclusion is inescapable that this Germany was the least well known to Stern and the chapter devoted to it the weakest in his autobiography.[151]

The description of events leading up to and including his fifth Germany, the reunified one after 1989, reads much like a travelogue. Stern was constantly on the move, flying back and forth across the Atlantic at least five or six times a year. Along the way he attended countless conferences and colloquia, lecturing here and there at various universities and other venues, mingling with a host of renowned celebrities, collecting droves of prizes, awards, and honorary degrees from fabled European institutions. In Germany he became *the* representative American historian, who excelled in presenting uncomfortable truths to adoring audiences with an insider's knowledge and an outsider's detachment. It is altogether fitting that the final chapter of his autobiography ends with a standing ovation for him at a televised ceremony in the historic Paulskirche in Frankfurt, where, after accepting the Peace Prize of the German Book Trade for 1999, he delivered a rousing oration about German inhumanity in the past and the need for liberal human rights everywhere in the future.[152]

A few episodes of this later period stood out. One was the extraordinary globe-trotting by Stern and his wife Peggy in the late 1970s, the result of a Ford Foundation traveling grant allowing an eighteen-month leave of absence from Columbia. If the premise of this award – that seeing other countries lacking in liberty would better enable Stern to understand the German past – was somewhat dubious, he certainly took every advantage of the freedom and generous finances. The list of destinations was long: Algeria, Egypt, the USSR, Poland, China, Japan, Latin America (Argentina, Brazil, Colombia), Sweden, and so on. Among the ports of call was also Israel, visited several times. A side benefit, after a lecture stop in Posen, was an opportunity to rent a car and drive to Wroclaw. Fritz Stern looked upon his former home of Breslau without emotion or attachment: "I felt like a stranger." More intriguing was a lecture tour in Red China, musing before a Shanghai audience about what lessons were to be learned from Bismarck and, characteristically, "catching a glimpse" of another culture and political system. Especially pleasing were a few months back in Paris, where Stern lived on the Quai des Fleurs hard by Notre Dame and lectured on European fascism at "Sciences Po" (formally, the Institut d'Études Politiques) in the Rue St.-Guillaume.[153]

But of course most of Stern's attention was riveted on Germany. His rising eminence led from one appointment to another. He became, for example, a trustee of the German Marshall Fund, a regular at the Biennial German-American Conference, and a member of the board of the Aspen Institute in Berlin. Consequently he met and chatted with everyone who was anyone in both political and academic circles. Even an abridged list is impressive: Pope John Paul II, Gershom Scholem, Simon Peres, Isaac Stern, Olaf Palme, Helmut Schmidt, Helmut Kohl, Carl-Friedrich and Richard von Weizsäcker, Hans Jüng, Rudolf Augstein, Joshka Fischer, George Soros, Richard Cheney, Richard Holbrooke, Isaiah Berlin, Raymond Aron, Gordon Craig, Jürgen Kocka, François Furet, Pierre Nora, Ernst Nolte, Jürgen Habermas. Most significantly and dearly for Stern, he became a life-long friend of Marion Dönhoff, publisher of *Die Zeit* and fellow vacation resident of their mutually beloved Sils Maria.[154]

Through it all Stern was developing what might be called his trademark historical theme about the "temptation" of National Socialism. In the course of doing so, as he later wrote, he found his voice in the German language: "an amalgam, perhaps, of older German prose to which I added a lighter American tone." This verbal facility was prominently on display at a ceremony on 17 June 1987 when Fritz Stern delivered the keynote address to an opening session of the West German Bundestag. His narration did not fail to note the thirteen interruptions for applause and a prolonged ovation at the conclusion. Visibly moved, Stern stood and sang with Chancellor Kohl and assembled parliamentary deputies the third verse of *Deutschland über alles*. This event, including the speech and its reception in the press, takes up fully ten pages of his autobiography.[155]

Fritz Stern properly attaches great importance to the *Mauerfall* of November 1989, "the brightest moment in Europe's darkest century." Emotionally he received news of Germany's post-Wall reunification with "optimistic equanimity," although while lecturing widely throughout both East and West he worried aloud about the economic imbalance of the nation's two parts.[156] This moderate skepticism was evident when he was invited by Margaret Thatcher to report on German affairs to British officials at Chequers. There he at least granted that circumstances now afforded Germany a "second chance." The same was true of his private life as he divorced his first wife and married Elisabeth Sifton. An operation for lower back trouble in 1991 and a mild heart attack soon thereafter did not appreciably slow him down, and he was able to recuperate both times successfully at his favorite spa of Sils Maria.[157] Highlight of the mid-1990s was a five-month appointment by Ambassador Richard Holbrooke to be a "senior adviser" at the US Embassy in Bonn (before its move back to Berlin). As noticed by *The New York Times*, Stern's "herringbone tweed jackets and wild white hair" contrasted in embassy corridors with the bustling young diplomats in their dark suits. Before leaving Bonn he took a memorable long walk along the Rhine beneath hills of the Siebengebirge, the sort of landscape to which his parents were once so attached: "I had never felt this kind of sympathetic contentment before." It seemed to represent "a new stage of reconciliation." Few other migrants from Germany before 1939 would be able to reach such a state of tranquil foregiveness.[158]

Stern retired from Columbia University in 1996 at the age of seventy, but his extensive agenda of lectures continued without pause: the Wannsee on the western edge of Berlin (with Henry Kissinger), Munich and Mainz, Israel, the Netherlands, Cambridge in England, and back to his native city with the Polish name of Wroclaw to receive the Silesian Cultural Award. During this time he expanded the third and last of his major historical works, *Einstein's German World*, for which the centerpiece was a lengthy essay on the collaboration and friendship of two genius types of modern German science, Albert Einstein and the man after whom Stern had been named, Fritz Haber.[159]

Toward the end of the decade Stern became involved in the so-called Goldhagen controversy, a highly publicized debate treating the reductionist charges of a young American political scientist that the entire phenomenon of the Holocaust could be ascribed to a congenital "eliminationist" mentality of the German people. Stern found these "contemptuous" attacks to be "odious" and said so in one of his typically forthright essays published in *Foreign Affairs*. It was, according to America's most esteemed expert on nineteenth-century Germany, Gordon Craig, "the best article I have read on the book and controversy."[160] The stage was thereby set for that singular distinction (the first for a historian) accorded to Stern at the Paulskirche in Frankfurt, just as the twenty-first century was about to begin. "I was stunned," he wrote. Perhaps so, but he was certainly well practiced in his role as the recipient of an award.[161]

A very short epilogue to the autobiography allows the recording of one more accolade, an honorary degree from the University of Wroclaw, complete with a performance of Beethoven's Ninth Symphony. After strains of the "Ode to Joy" had faded, Stern arose with his accustomed aplomb and pointed frankness to express thanks to the city "in which I was nurtured and from which I was expelled."[162] It remains only for the good burghers of his old hometown to erect a statue to Fritz Stern with this epitaph etched on its pedestal.

Chapter Six

FIVE WHO FLED

The migration of numerous European intellectuals to the United States in the 1930s forms a huge and complex backdrop before which the story of the five subjects in this volume must be set. Even when confined to those who left Germany, the list of luminaries is remarkable, stretching from the incomparable Albert Einstein, who enjoyed a long celebrity at Princeton, to the severely troubled playwright Ernst Toller, who committed suicide alone in a New York hotel room. Other prominent names come quickly to mind: authors of fiction like Thomas Mann and Carl Zuckmayer; political scientists Hans Morgenthau, Arnold Bergsträsser, and Hannah Arendt; sociologists Theodor Adorno and Max Horkheimer from the Frankfurt School; psychologists Erich Fromm, Karen Horney, and Erik Erikson; painters Max Ernst, Joseph Albers, and Georg Gross; musical composers from Paul Hindemith to Kurt Weill, as well as the conductors Bruno Walter and Otto Klemperer; architects Walter Gropius and Mies van der Rohe; and so forth. Nothing of the dimension or quality of this intellectual sea change has occurred before or since, and it is surely worthwhile to attempt to bring the record of it up to date.

As noted in the preface, the five scholars selected here have been arranged according to the chronological order of their birth. This sequence by age makes perfect sense especially when one considers the emotional impact of emigration. Probably the least deeply affected were the eldest and the youngest. Felix Gilbert was in 1933 an adult whose professional career was already launched and who, after a brief interruption for military service in the American army, could successfully continue on that academic path in the New World. He did so of course in the context of a university life that was secure and welcoming not only for him but to dozens of other displaced persons. By contrast, Fritz Stern left Breslau when he was a small boy who had barely had a chance to observe Nazi Germany and who grew into manhood as an American teenager fully acclimated and linguistically proficient. Those for whom the transition from Germany to America was manifestly more trying were the three born around 1920: Klemens von Klemperer (1916), Werner T. Angress (1920), and Peter Gay (1923). They consciously experienced the end of the Weimar Republic and the beginnings of an increasingly oppressive domination by National Socialism. In that agonizing process, given all the fluctuations and ambiguities of the time, two striking events stood out: the proclamation of the Nazi racial laws at Nürnberg in 1935 and the shocking violence of *Kristallnacht* in November 1938. Whatever illusions these three and their families may have held about belonging to the German nation were completely vitiated in the space of those three years, and accordingly the attempt to escape from Europe began to crowd out all other thoughts.

The date and circumstances of their departure were also significant. In this regard Gilbert and Klemperer were the most fortunate. Both had international connections that facilitated their flight to freedom. And they left early. Gilbert's stay in London from 1933 to 1936 was not altogether pleasant, but it made clear to him that his best option was a move to America, made possible by temporary academic appointments in California and at Princeton. Klemperer, after a brief abortive stop at Oxford, found refuge in 1934 with part of his family in Vienna, thus avoiding the troubled years of Nazi *Gleichschaltung* in Germany until Austria's absorption into the Third Reich. Neither of them was therefore a direct witness to Germany's dark years in the late 1930s – exception made for Klemperer's coincidental presence in Berlin during *Kristallnacht* – a spectacle that long haunted Angress, Gay, and Stern. Stern sailed for the United States at the end of September 1938, Gay in April 1939, and Angress not until October 1939 after the Eastern war in Europe had already begun in Poland. They were thus among the last wave to be released from Germany before the opening of hostilities in France and the Lowlands in early May 1940, which seriously diminished any further opportunity for escape.

The means to finance a safe passage by ship to the United States was obviously crucial. Migration to America in the 1930s was not for the poor, and it is strikingly uniform that all of the families in the group of five were well grounded in the middle-class wealth of Germany's *Bildungbürgertum*. Undoubtedly the richest were Gilbert and Klemperer, both of whom had relatives very recently ennobled but whose fortune derived mainly from bourgeois business and banking interests. From a long line of Breslau physicians, Fritz Stern likewise stood to inherit a substantial estate. His autobiographical account offers no suggestion that his family had any difficulty in affording whatever travel arrangements could be booked. Angress and Gay ranked much lower on the social and financial scale. Yet both of these families could at one time or another afford to engage household servants, and they were certainly not indigent at the moment when obtaining rail travel and sea passage became critical. In sum, money and connections were indispensable for departure. Thus the five, each in a somewhat distinct fashion, were illustrative of this fundamental verity.

Obviously enough, all had some Jewish element in their family background. That was, after all, the operative reason for the urgency of leaving Germany. Yet, to repeat an earlier observation, it would be a mistake to assume without qualification that we are dealing here simply with five Jews. Although the Nazi Party chose to classify them as such, they themselves did not. Gilbert's remark that he was only one quarter Jewish was indicative, apart from the fact that many of his forebears like Felix Mendelssohn had converted to Christianity generations before. Both Klemperer and Stern were baptized at birth as Lutherans, and they grew up in homes where Jewish tradition was inconspicuous or non-existent. Christmas and Easter were the major family celebrations. The New Testament was a holy scripture. Sunday was the day to attend religious services – of course in a church rather than a synagogue. Angress and Gay were undoubtedly closest to Judaism, but even they had a thoroughly secular upbringing. Angress accepted the ceremony of bar mitzvah (as Gay did not); yet he attached little religious significance to it, and throughout his adult life he remained stoutly agnostic. Indeed, he was never free of the most common form of Berlin anti-Semitism that was directed against Orthodox Jewry in the early twentieth century. Peter Gay was still more radical in his rejection of a Jewish identity, passing childhood as he did in a family that was outright hostile to religion in any form. His memoirs hence echo the refrain of all the others by explaining how the events after 1933 suddenly created for him the unsought status of a German Jew. Before then, what he and the others most conspicuously shared was not religion but nationality. They were German, as Angress put it, to the core. If there was an exception, perhaps, it was Klemperer, whose claim to distinctiveness, however, rested on his family connection to Austria, not to Judaism.

Integration into American society proved in no instance to be a serious problem. All five protagonists married American women, and each of them came to enjoy a distinguished academic career within the broad and flexible American university system. Although their scholarly focus varied, all of their work was deeply informed by the experience of Weimar and Nazi Germany. Felix Gilbert strayed farthest from his Central European past by pursuing studies of Renaissance Italy. Yet it is not at all far-fetched to view his publications on Machiavelli and the Roman papacy as a commentary on the bellicosity and devious statecraft that he had witnessed in his own time. Besides, he added to his bibliography three works on modern Europe. Gay also concentrated mostly on another country, in his case France. Without question he did so in part as an expression of his early rejection of all things German. Yet he conceived his first book on a topic concerning pre-1914 Germany, and he later brought out a well considered analysis of interwar German intellectuals who represented a prelude to Nazism. The German Enlightenment and the German bourgeoisie were also among the objects of his investigation. Klemperer, Angress, and Stern devoted themselves more exclusively to studies of the German past. Each of them began a scholarly career by exploring the origins of Nazism, and they later branched out into other topics directly or indirectly related to that common starting-point. Naturally there is no objective way to measure the individual or collective impact of these historians as writers, teachers, and colleagues in their chosen profession. Still, it is no empty act of piety to remark once more how deep and wide was the enrichment of American scholarship through the chaotic migration from fascist Europe in the 1930s. It was Hitler's greatest gift to the United States.

It might appear a curiosity that the Holocaust figures hardly at all in these five autobiographical accounts, and the evidence is sparse that their authors regarded themselves as victims. In a few cases the Nazi destruction of European Jews came close to home: the father of Werner Angress, for instance, and one of Fritz Stern's aunts, both of whom perished at Auschwitz. Yet the most persistently shared feeling was resentment about an unjust rejection. All of the five had been loyal and patriotic Germans before their expulsion and before (as Klemperer wrote) they discovered a second *Heimat* in the United States. They returned to Germany only to find, without surprise, that they no longer belonged there. Even Tom Angress, the only one to settle again in Berlin after the war, found it difficult to warm up to those Germans who had remained in their homeland and who had continued, for the most part, to support the Nazi regime to the war's end. Nostalgia is decidedly not the appropriate term to describe the feelings of those ostracized from German society. In this sense, even when unmentioned, the stench of the Holocaust does hang over all five testimonies.

Inevitably, for those who had fled, their subsequent return to Germany was not without some emotional baggage. By far the most dramatic reappearance was that of Tom Angress, in an American army uniform, parachuted into combat. As a genuine war hero, wounded and decorated, he saw at first hand the reality of what had occurred under Nazi rule, including the concentration camps. In this experience there must have been some kind of catharsis that permitted him, many years later, to take up residence again in Berlin and to set out his recollections in the German language. That intimately detailed record clearly stands apart from the others. The two elders, Gilbert and Klemperer, also served in the U.S. military, but as OSS officers behind the lines. Neither saw battle. What they did see was the widespread destruction and wreckage left right after the war, macabre signs of the terrible beating absorbed by the German people in their cities during 1944 and 1945. Yet they also became witnesses to the German recovery and eventual rehabilitation. Personal contacts mattered enormously in this evolution, and the international community of scholars did its part to patch up wounds of the past and to reestablish cordial relations between postwar Germany and the United States. The two youngsters, Peter Gay and Fritz Stern, were spared any exposure to the violence of wartime. Paradoxically – or perhaps not – they were probably the most emotionally upset by revisiting scenes of their childhood. Both initially hesitated to return to Germany. Gay did not see Berlin again until 1961 and Stern did not stand before his boyhood home in Breslau until the end of the 1970s. Both retained the feeling of being foreigners in Germany, and both confessed as adults to harboring some hatred in their heart because of their earlier inglorious exit. Without a doubt, Peter Gay's negative reactions to postwar Germany were the most pronounced and remained to some extent unresolved. Much better known in Germany, as well as more frequently and publicly honored there, Fritz Stern finally achieved a degree of reconciliation that was unmatched.

All in all, then, this is a tale with a happy ending, an anthology about overcoming adversity and a tribute to those who endured. There was something indomitable about these five who fled from Nazi Germany and who found a new identity in America. Not every refugee from war and persecution fared so well, we know, but it is nonetheless gratifying to learn that, even under the most drastic of circumstances, human survival is sometimes possible.

Endnotes

1   H. Stuart Hughes, *The Sea Change. The Migration of Social Thought, 1930-1965* (New York, 1975). See also Franz Neumann et al., *The Cultural Migration: The European Scholar in America* (Philadelphia, 1953); Donald Peterson Kent, *The Refugee Intellectual: The Americanization of the Immigrants of 1933-41* (New York, 1953); Helge Pross, *Die Deutsche Akademische Emigration nach den Vereinigten Staaten 1933-1941* (Berlin, 1955); Laura Fermi, *Illustrious Immigrants: The Intellectual Migration from Europe 1930-1941* (Chicago, 1968); Volker Berghahn, "Deutschlandbilder 1945-1965. Angloamerikanische Historiker und moderne deutsche Geschichte," in Ernst Schulin (ed.), *Deutsche Geschichtswissenschaft nach dem Zweiten Weltkrieg (1945-1965)* (Munich, 1969), pp. 239-72; Donald Fleming and Bernard Bailyn (eds.), *The Intellectual Migration from Germany to America* (Cambridge, Mass., 1969); Martin Jay, *Permament Exiles. Essays on the Intellectual Migration from Germany to America* (New York, 1985); Kenneth D. Barkin, "German Émigré Historians in America: the Fifties, Sixties, and Seventies," in Hartmut Lehmann and James J. Sheehan (eds.), *An Interrupted Past. German-Speaking Refugee Historians in the United*

States after 1933 (Cambridge, 1991); and Jeremy D. Popkin, *History, Historians, and Autobiography* (Chicago, 2005).

2   Catherine Epstein, *A Past Renewed. A Catalog of German-Speaking Refugee Historians in the United States after 1933* (Cambridge, 1993). See also her summary essay, "Schicksalsgeschichte: Refugee Historians in the United States," in Lehmann and Sheehan (eds.), *An Interrupted Past*, pp. 116-35. Another comment on the "significant brain drain" from Germany of those who had already joined the historical profession before their emigration is by Wolfgang Mommsen, "German Historiography during the Weimar Republic and the Émigré Historians," ibid., pp. 32-66.

3   Heinz Wolf, *Deutsch-jüdische Emigrationshistoriker in den USA und der Nationalsozialismus* (Bern, 1988).

4   Felix Gilbert, *A European Past: Memoirs 1905-1945* (New York and London, 1988), pp. 45-46. A German edition was published as *Lehrjahre im alten Europa. Erinnerungen 1905-1945* (Berlin, 1989).

5   Gilbert, *A European Past*, pp. 59-60.

6   Ibid., pp. 6-11.

7   Ibid., pp. 13-19.

8   Ibid., pp. 20-24.

9   Ibid., pp. 4, 34-39.

10   Ibid., pp. 41-42.

11   Ibid., pp. 44-49.

12   Ibid., pp. 50-52. Notably, Holborn was the author of a *History of Modern Germany* (3 vols.; New York, 1959-1969). See Gerhard A. Ritter, "Die emigrierten Meinecke-Schüler in den Vereinigten Staaten. Leben und

Geschichtsschreibung im Spannungsfeld zwischen Deutschland und der neuen Heimat: Hajo Holborn, Felix Gilbert, Dietrich Gerhard, Hans Rosenberg," *Historische Zeitschrift* 284 (2007): 59-102; and Otto Pflanze, "The Americanization of Hajo Holborn," in Lehmann and Shechan (eds.), *An Interrupted Past*, pp. 170-79.

13 Gilbert, *A European Past*, pp. 52-53, 64-65.

14 Ibid., pp. 59, 65-66.

15 See the essay by Ritter cited in footnote 12. Hans Rosenberg was doubtless a more influential historian than Gilbert, especially in promoting modern German social and economic history. But he left no full-scale memoir, only a sketch: "Rückblick auf ein Historikerleben zwischen zwei Kulturen," in *Machteliten und Wirtschaftskonjunkturen. Studien zur neueren deutschen Sozial- und Wirtschaftsgeschichte* (Göttingen, 1978). See Hanna Schissler, "Explaining History: Hans Rosenberg," in Lehmann and Sheehan (eds.), *An Interrupted Past*, pp. 180-87; and Gerhard A. Ritter, "Hans Rosenberg, 1904-1988," *Geschichte und Gesellschaft* 15 (1989): 282-302.

16 Gilbert, *A European Past*, pp. 68-70, 72-75. See the monograph by Gilbert, *Johann Gustav Droysen und die preussisch-deutsche Frage* (Munich, 1931); and his edition of *Johann Gustav Droysen: Politische Schriften* (Berlin and Munich, 1933).

17 Gilbert, *A European Past*, pp. 70-71, 77-79, 92-97.

18 Ibid., pp. 85-89.

19 Ibid., pp. 119-24.

20 Ibid., pp. 158-74.

21 Ibid., pp. 175-77.

22 Ibid., pp. 177-79.

23 Ibid., pp. 185-87. See Barry M. Katz, "German Historians in the Office of Strategic Services," in Lehmann and Sheehan (eds.), *An Interrupted Past*, pp. 136-39.

24 Gilbert, *A European Past*, pp. 188-89, 194-201.

25 Ibid., pp. 200-201, 215.

26 Ibid., pp. 205-209.

27 Ibid., pp. 212-14.

28 Ibid., pp. 217-20.

29 See Barbara Miller Lane, "Felix Gilbert at Bryn Mawr College," in Hartmut Lehmann (ed.), *Felix Gilbert as Scholar and Teacher* (Washington, D.C., 1992), pp. 11-16.

30 See Gilbert, *Machiavelli and Guicciardini: Politics and History in Sixteenth-Century Florence* (Princeton, 1965); and *The Pope, His Banker, and Venice* (Cambridge, Mass., 1980). Regarding the twentieth century, he edited *Hitler Directs His War* (New York, 1950), and with Gordon A. Craig, *The Diplomats 1919-1939* (New York, 1953), in addition to writing a textbook, *The End of the European Era. 1890 to the Present* (New York, 1970).

31 Klemens von Klemperer, *Voyage Through the Twentieth Century: A Historian's Recollections and Reflections* (New York and Oxford, 2009), p. 9

32 Ibid., pp. 9-11.

33 Ibid., pp. 6, 9-10.

34 Ibid., pp. 3, 6.

35 Ibid., p. 7.

36 Ibid., pp. 12-16.

37 Ibid., pp. 17-19.

38 Ibid., p. 20.

39 Ibid., pp. 21-24, 27, 29-32.

40 Ibid., pp. 33-35.

41 Ibid., pp. 36-44.

42 Ibid., pp. 46-53.

43 Ibid., pp. 54-59.

44 Ibid., pp. 59-60.

45 Ibid., pp. 61-63.

46 Ibid., pp. 64-66.

47 Ibid., pp. 67-78. See Klemperer, *Germany's New Conservatism: Its History and Dilemma in the Twentieth Century* (Princeton, 1957).

48 Klemperer, *Voyage Through the Twentieth Century*, pp. 78-81.

49 Ibid., pp. 82-86. See Klemperer, *Ignaz Seipel: Christian Statesman in a Time of Crisis* (Princeton, 1972).

50 Klemperer, *Voyage Through the Twentieth Century*, pp. 87-92.

51 Ibid., pp. 93-99. See Klemperer, *German Resistance against Hitler: The Search for Allies Abroad, 1938-1945* (Oxford, 1992).

52 Klemperer, *Voyage Through the Twentieth Century*, pp. 106-11.

53 Ibid., pp. 116-19.

54 Ibid., p. 137.

55 Ibid.

56 Ibid., pp. 115-16, 133.

57 Werner T. Angress, … *immer etwas abseits. Jugenderinnerungen eines jüdischen Berliners 1920-1945* (Berlin, 2005).

58 Ibid., pp. 6-12.

59 Ibid., pp. 12-16.

60 Ibid., pp. 18-22.

61 Ibid., pp. 19, 28-33.

62 Ibid., pp. 36-38.

63 Ibid., pp. 39-46.

64 Ibid., pp. 49-50.

65 Ibid., pp. 54-60.

66 Ibid., pp. 60-62, 66.

67 Ibid., pp. 69-74.

68 Ibid., pp. 78-80.

69 Ibid., pp. 81-86.

70 Ibid., pp. 86-88.

71 Ibid., pp. 89-97.

72 Ibid., pp. 99-125.

73 Ibid., pp. 126-58. His adventures at Gross Breesen and his appreciation of Curt Bondy are related in Angress, *Generation zwischen Furcht und Hoffnung: Jüdische Jugend im Dritten Reich*, published in Germany in 1985 and then in English as *Between Fear and Hope: Jewish Youth in the Third Reich* (New York, 1988).

74 Angress, … *immer etwas abseits*, pp. 159-77.

75 Ibid., pp. 178-200.

76 Ibid., pp. 201-206, 211-12.

77 Ibid., pp. 206-29.

78 Ibid., pp. 230-48.

79 Ibid., pp. 251-56, 262-78.

80 Ibid., pp. 278-86.

81 Ibid., pp. 291-97, 301.

82 Ibid., p. 307.

83 Ibid., pp. 308-309, 312-14.

84 Ibid., pp. 311, 314-15.

85 Ibid., pp. 316-19.

86 Ibid., pp. 320-29.

87   Ibid., pp. 330-35.

88   See Angress, *Stillborn Revolution: The Communist Bid for Power in Germany, 1921-1923* (Princeton, 1963).

89   See, for instance, Angress, "Juden im politischen Leben der Revolutionszeit," *Deutsches Judentum in Krieg und Revolution 1916-1923* [Schriftenreihe Wissenschaftlicher Abhandlungen des Leo Baeck Instituts 25] (Tübingen, 1971), pp. 137-315; "'Between Baden and Luxemburg.' Jewish Socialists on the Eve of the First World War," *Year Book XXII of the Leo Baeck Institute* (London, 1977), pp. 3-34; and "The German Army's *Judenzählung*' of 1916. Genesis – Consequences – Significance," *Year Book XXIII of the Leo Baeck Institute* (London, 1978), pp. 117-37.

90   Peter Gay, *My German Question: Growing Up in Nazi Berlin* (New Haven and London, 1998), pp. x-xii, 99. A German edition has been published as *Meine deutsche Frage: Jugend in Berlin 1933-1939* (Munich, 1999).

91   Gay, *My German Question*, pp. 22-24, 32.

92   Ibid., pp. ix, 24-25, 35, 178.

93   Ibid., pp. x, 8-9, 17-18.

94   Ibid., pp. 40-41.

95   Ibid., pp. 62-64.

96   Ibid., pp. 61-62.

97   Ibid., pp. 19-20, 75-76.

98   Ibid., pp. 47-53.

99   Ibid., pp. 55-56.

100 Ibid., pp. 54-55.

101 Ibid., pp. 78-83, 95-106, 117-18.

102 Ibid., pp. 30-31, 67, 108-10.

103 Ibid., pp. 111-13.

104 Ibid., pp. 114, 119-20.

105 Ibid., pp. 122-23, 131-34.

106 Ibid., pp. 123, 130-31, 138-40, 143-44.

107 Ibid., pp. 149-51.

108 Ibid., pp. 152-53.

109 Ibid., pp. 154-59.

110 Ibid., pp. 159-75, 180-83.

111 Ibid., pp. 21-22, 190-91. See Gay, *The Dilemma of Democratic Socialism: Eduard Bernstein's Challenge to Marx* (New York, 1952).

112 Gay, *My German Question*, pp. 1-6, 184-93.

113 Ibid., pp. 11-13.

114 See Gay, *The Party of Humanity: Essays in the French Enlightenment* (New York, 1964); *The Enlightenment: An Interpretation* (2 vols.; New York, 1966-1969); *Weimar Culture: The Outsider as Insider* (New York, 1968).

115 Gay, *My German Question*, pp. 196-99.

116 Ibid., pp. 199-202. See Gay, *Freud, Jews, and Other Germans: Masters and Victims in Modernist Culture* (New York, 1978); *Freud for Historians* (New York, 1985); A *Godless Jew: Freud, Atheism, and the Making of Psychoanalysis* (New Haven and London, 1987); *Freud: A Life for Our Time* (New York, 1988); *Reading Freud: Explorations and Entertainments* (New Haven and London, 1990); and *The Bourgeois Experience: Victoria to Freud* (5 vols.; New York, 1984-1998).

117 Fritz Stern, *Five Germanys I Have Known* (New York, 2006). A German edition has been published as *Fünf Deutschland und ein Leben: Erinnerungen* (Munich, 2007).

118 Stern, *Five Germanys*, pp. 13-17.

119 Ibid., pp. 17-32.

120 Ibid., pp. 34-50.

121 Ibid., pp. 51-52, 56-79.

122 Ibid., pp. 82-86.

123 Ibid., pp. 86-88.

124 Ibid., pp. 89-94

125 Ibid., pp. 101-104.

126 Ibid., pp. 98-101, 107.

127 Ibid., pp. 105-12.

128 Ibid., pp. 113-22.

129 Ibid., pp. 123-24.

130 Ibid., pp. 125-26.

131 Ibid., pp. 126-30.

132 Ibid., pp. 131-38.

133 Ibid., pp. 138-39, 148-49, 153.

134 Ibid., pp. 154-56.

135 Ibid., pp. 156-63.

136 Ibid., pp. 164-67.

137 Ibid., pp. 168-93.

138 Ibid., pp. 194-95.

139 Ibid., pp. 195-99.

140 Ibid., pp. 199-200.

141 Ibid., pp. 208-11.

142 Ibid., pp. 225-28. See Stern, *The Politics of Cultural Despair: A Study in the Rise of the Germanic Ideology* (New York, 1961).

143 Stern, *Five Germanys*, pp. 225-26.

144 Ibid., pp. 228-32.

145 Ibid., pp. 232-35.

146 Ibid., pp. 236-38.

147 Ibid., pp. 241-44.

148 Ibid., pp. 245-61.

149 Ibid., pp. 276, 282, 293-95.

150 Ibid., pp. 295-99. See Stern, *Gold and Iron. Bismarck, Bleichröder, and the Building of the German Empire* (New York, 1977); and my review in *Central European History* 10 (1977): 165-71.

151 Stern, *Five Germanys*, pp. 304-43.

152 Ibid., p. 514.

153 Ibid., pp. 346-98.

154 Ibid., pp. 261-63, 391, 399-423.

155 Ibid., pp. 424-29, 440-51.

156 Ibid., pp. 457-59.

157 Ibid., pp. 466-69, 474-76.

158 Ibid., pp. 481-98.

159 Ibid., pp. 500-504. See Stern, *Einstein's German World* (New York, 1998).

160 Stern, *Five Germanys*, pp. 506-508.

161 Ibid., pp. 509-14.

162 Ibid., pp. 517-20.

SUGGESTED FURTHER
SECONDARY READING

Epstein, Catherine. *A Past Renewed. A Catalog of German-Speaking Refugee Historians in the United States after 1933*. Cambridge, 1993.

Fermi, Laura. *Illustrious Immigrants: The Intellectual Migration from Europe 1930-1941*. Chicago, 1968.

Fleming, Donald, and Bernard Bailyn (eds.). *The Intellectual Migration from Gemany to America*. Cambridge, Mass., 1969.

Hughes, H. Stuart. *The Sea Change. The Migration of Social Thought, 1930-1965*. New York, 1975.

Jay, Martin. *Permanent Exiles. Essays on the Intellectual Migration from Germany to America*. New York, 1985.

Kent, Donald Peterson. *The Refugee Intellectual: The Americanization of the Immigrants of 1933-41*. New York, l953.

Lehmann, Hartmut (ed.). *Felix Gilbert as Scholar and Teacher*. Washington, D.C., 1992.

Lehmann, Hartmut, and James J. Sheehan (eds.). *An Interrupted Past. German-Speaking Refugee Historians in the United States after 1933*. Cambridge, 1991.

Neumann, Franz, et al. *The Cultural Migration: The European Scholar in America*. Philadelphia, 1953.

Popkin, Jeremy D. *History, Historians, and Autobiography*. Chicago, 2005.

Pross, Helge. *Die Deutsche Akademische Emigration nach den Vereinigten Staaten 1933-1941*. Berlin, 1955.

Schulin, Ernst (ed.). *Deutsche Geschichtswissenschaft nach dem Zweiten Weltkrieg (1945-1965)*. Munich, 1969.

Wolf, Heinz. *Deutsch-jüdische Emigrationshistoriker in den USA und der Nationalsozialismus*. Bern, 1988.

NAME INDEX

SUBJECT INDEX

Koblenz, 48

Kristallnacht, 19, 52, 65, 79-80

Landsberg, 7

Landwehrkanal (Berlin), 4

Latin America, 74

League of Nations, 9

Left Bank (Paris), 11

Leipzig, 48

Leo Baeck Institute, 44

Leuna chemical works, 72

liberalism, 5, 12, 67

Lisbon, 53

Liverpool, 39

London, 9, 11, 21, 31, 37, 68, 80

Long Island, 43

Louvre, 11

Lowlands. *See* Belgium, Netherlands

Lutheranism, 2, 17, 59-60, 81

Mainz, 76

Manhattan, 65-66

Mannheim, 5

Marburg, 22

Maryland, 39

Mauerfall of 1989. *See* Berlin Wall

medical profession, 1-2, 49, 59, 62-63, 65-66, 81

Merseburg, 72

middle class. *See* bourgeoisie

Mittelstand. See bourgeoisie

Munich, 7, 24, 52, 76

Murnau, 24

nationalism, 4, 30, 36, 66, 82. *See also* patriotism

Naumburg, 72

Nazism, 1-2, 5-7, 9-10, 12, 17, 19, 23-24, 26-27, 32-36, 39, 42, 44-45, 47-48, 51, 53-55, 58, 61, 63, 65, 67-68, 72, 75, 79-85

Nazi-Soviet pact of 1939, 66

Netherlands, 4, 37, 40, 48, 64, 66, 76, 80

Neuilly, 62

New England, 25, 67

Newport, 20

New York, 19, 38, 44, 65, 78

New York Times, 76

Nijmegen, 40

Nikolassee, 6

Nobel prize, 60

nobility. *See* aristocracy